KATAHDIN
(*With Love*):
An Inspirational Journey

KATAHDIN
(*With Love*):
An Inspirational Journey

MADELAINE CORNELIUS

Milton Publishing Company, Inc.
P. O. Box 6
Lookout Mountain, Tennessee 37350

Printed by Arcata Graphics
Kingsport, Tennessee 37662

ISBN 0-924234-25-3

ACKNOWLEDGEMENTS

I wish to express appreciation to all our family and friends for their enthusiastic encouragement during our hike and during my writing; I again thank my brother, Bob Tolle, and his wife, Elaine, for helping to make our reentry to our modern world as gentle as possible; to publicly praise the volunteers who faithfully help to maintain the Appalachian Trail and to all those who believed in my manuscript.

To My Husband

Thank you for always believing in me, loving me,
listening to me and helping me.

FOREWORD

Each day, upon our return home and to our former roles as a foundry supervisor and a nurse, a love note was tucked into my lunchbag by my husband. His comical but realistic pencil sketch depicted us somewhere along the Appalachian Trail, beginning in Georgia and ending in Maine. His printed message precisely described our experience on that particular day. Most important, though, his love for me, his wife and wildflower, was perceived.

These notes evoked vivid memories from our six-month journey together. The poignant lessons learned on the trail aptly apply to our present lives in our modern world.

Herein are my Mountain Man's words to me, along with my feelings and impressions recorded daily in my journal on our two-thousand-mile hike over some of the oldest mountains on earth.

Day by Day

My mental conflict persisted throughout the night. Agonizing, I vainly attempted to resolve my dilemma. Wanting desperately to finish hiking the entire Appalachian Trail with Gene, I acknowledged the fact that my pace was too slow for us to reach Katahdin together before the ice and snow came.

All the painful episodes of the past five and a half months fleetingly surfaced — my fears, the tragedy, my fall in Pennsylvania, my abscessed tooth and my stiff knees. What compelled me to keep going? Thoughts — the wonderful funny times we shared, the mountain peaks we climbed over, the storms we weathered, the secrets of nature revealed to us, the people whose lives touched ours — came rushing into my mind. As always, Katahdin (Ka ta' din), the final peak, beckoned us, calling us, challenging us. The time had come to reach a crucial decision but first we needed to share our deepest feelings with one another.

In sharing, our story came into focus.

March 31, 1981 Georgia

'Together, with desire, most anything can be accomplished.'

Sprinkled with scintillating stars, the night sky flung a bejeweled canopy over us. We stood together, silent, with our arms around one another, on the threshold of a new and simple lifestyle. The magnitude of our adventure was at last apparent to us.

The two of us were all alone. Our tent was erected in Big Stamp Gap, several miles beyond the summit of Springer Mountain, Georgia. All our food was stuffed into a bag and hung high between two trees. Our backpacks with rain covers in place were propped against a tree.

Suddenly the world seemed larger and all at once I felt smaller. This feeling of minuteness intensified during the night when rolling thunder, flashes of lightning, and driving rain awakened us.

April 1

'Thank you, honey, for your love and, Lord, for the beginning of a new day. Keep smiling.'

As we were busy organizing ourselves, a male hiker called to us, "Which way to Maine?" Gene yelled, "Take a left and follow the white blazes." By nine-fifty we got underway, agreeing that we'd do better the next morning.

The hiking was not difficult as the trail followed fire roads and old logging roads, ideal for conditioning us gradually. Around noon, the sun broke through and the sky turned blue. Noontootla Creek, formed by the convergence of three mountain streams, looked crystal clear in the sunlight.

We had determined in our planning stage to eat our main meal mid-afternoon, thereby giving ourselves a longer chance to rest. Our suppers would be something quick and easy to fix. Today's meal was freeze-dried shrimp creole that had numerous small shrimp in zesty sauce on rice. When it was time to do K.P., Gene grabbed a handful of moss to scrub out our cooking pot and dishes. Grinning, he demonstrated that the moss worked as well as brillo.

The hike up Hawk Mountain was not as steep as anticipated and Hawk Mountain Shelter became home our second night out. A shallow, wooden, three-sided structure with a wooden platform for sleeping, it proved conducive to stargazing.

Don Farrell, a retired geological surveyor, and Jeff, about nineteen, were already there. We talked and arranged our sleeping bags before going down to the stream, where fresh deer tracks were imprinted in the soft earth.

While sipping a cup of hot tea, I wrote an entry in the trail register. A copy book, it had a written invitation for hikers to sign it, to express one's feelings or thoughts, write poetry or sketch a picture. There was also a request for the last one having space in the book to pack it out and send it to the person listed on the front. A promise to reimburse the sender accompanied the request. These registers, we learned later on, formed a vital link in trail communications. Reading the entries, it was apparent that most of the hikers used trail names. For example, Don signed his entry "The Cape Codder." Months passed, however, before we adopted trail names.

April 2

'Time out to rest will help me and my friend to gain most from the day. I love you.'

Leaving by seven-thirty, we verbally patted ourselves on the back. There wasn't a cloud in the sky and Gene's tiny thermometer registered 48 degrees. Having hiked into Horses' Gap, we began the steep ascent up Sassafras Mountain, where violets and chickweed grew in clusters at the lower elevations. It was here Gene caught sight of a red fox darting across the path. Descending steeply into Cooper Gap and climbing up Justus Mountain, my pack gradually became heavier on my bony shoulders, as if someone kept adding bricks. Tightening my waistband, I attempted to transfer most of the weight onto my hips.

Justus Creek at the base of Justus Mountain enticed us to stop for dinner and soak our feet in the ice cold waters. Fortunately, our boots needed no breaking in and felt comfortable. There, resting in the sunshine, we lost track of time as we talked with each other and another through-hiker called Grady, who had arrived shortly afterwards. Travelling solo, he told us of his pregnant wife and young child, whom he missed very much. Believing mental readiness is the key to successfully hiking the trail, we wondered, after listening, if this was the right time for him to be starting out. Gene feels a person will eventually be physically conditioned by the trail but must begin psychologically prepared or else be easily defeated.

At Gooch Gap Lean-to, a hooting owl effectively announced bedtime. By this time I had two sore shoulders and two very sore hips.

April 3

Starting out at sunrise, our aching bodies felt slightly improved after a night's rest. Along the way, a solitary white bloodroot, proudly protruding from amongst dry leaves, heralded springtime. Gene carefully focused our Minolta camera, recording the powerful message of this tiny bloom. The camera hung in readiness on Gene's chest, suspended by a strap attached to his packframe, keeping it off his neck. Two and a half pounds of camera seemed reasonable while sitting on a soft sofa at home planning for our trip. On the trail it proved to be an extravagant necessity, as we wished to document our journey with fine close-ups as well as distance pictures.

Towards the end of the day, my body inwardly screamed to stop, although my spirit was eager to keep going. Every moveable part of my anatomy hurt and I became acutely aware of muscles that I never noticed before. Gene moved right along without any outward difficulty. I found myself straining forward going uphill, breathing hard — my pulse pounding. Concentrated effort was required to put one foot in front of the other, until at last we came to a level area in a grove of bare hardwood trees. Unbuckling my waistbelt, Gene lifted my pack off my sore shoulders. Immediately, my shoulders began to rise of their own accord, as if they were detached from my body.

My clothes were dirty, my hands felt grubby and my body ached, but within, I felt content. It was time to rest.

April 4

'A treat will come to you when you least expect it. I love you.'

The morning air was damp and heavy with mist, creating an aura of mystery in the woods. Tripping over a small stump, my walking stick went flying like a baton. Gene heard the thud and hurried back to assist me. Bruised and dirtied, I realized the earth was beginning to mold me. My beige mittens, the last of my clean items of clothing, were brown with dirt.

Going up Blood Mountain by switchbacks, we again met "The Cape Codder," who was now travelling with Grady and Howard, a middle-aged hiker whom we met for the first time.

On top of Blood Mountain stood a stone structure, somber looking on the outside, and dreary and damp on the inside. Sheets of discolored, torn plastic hung over some of the windows and noisily flapped in the wind. The two rooms had a dirt floor and were vacant. On this type of day, it was eerie and uninviting.

Coming down into Neel's Gap, we were delighted to find a backpacker's store. Hurrying in, my first question was, "Do you sell ice cream?" The proprietor replied, "I have Nutty Buddies." Elated, I responded, "I'll take two. Rather, make that three, as my husband will want one, too."

Many times we have laughed about my selfish "two for me and one for you" response to this surprise.

April 5

We camped a mile off the trail behind the new Whitley Gap Shelter, which was already crowded by the time we arrived. Lying awake for hours, I listened to the night sounds, all seemingly magnified. The tall trees squeaked in the wailing winds and my legs ached from lactic acid buildup. Sometime during the night, rain began to fall, continuing into daylight. Consequently, we got off to a slow start and decided to make it a very short hiking day, covering only five and six-tenths miles.

The sun was shining by the time we reached Low Gap Shelter at two o'clock in the afternoon. Howard, Grady, and

"The Cape Codder" were already there. Everyone hung their wet things out to dry in the stiff breezes whipping through the gap. Gene helped me to shampoo my hair by pouring ice cold water over my head, resulting in loud squeals and a numb brain. Quickly, the sun and breezes dried my hair to a new sheen and I felt marvelous.

Retiring early, I never heard a sound.

April 6

Today was Gene's fiftieth birthday and we were "high on life." The weather was perfect for hiking — blue skies, cold and clear. Skin moisturizer was the one thing I neglected to bring and our faces became red and stiff from the sun and wind.

Walking along I collected a bouquet of dried flowers for Gene's birthday gift. The brittle flowers were all shades of brown to cream-color with some as fragile as the finest crystal. This is the first time it ever occurred to me to give my husband flowers for his birthday; here in the woods it seemed appropriate.

Lunching in Unicoi Gap, we decided upon crackers with cheese and dried fruit, as our water was low. About a mile uphill, a stream crossed the trail and we replenished our canteens.

We intended to try to reach Montray Shelter on Tray Mountain where our new acquaintances were planning on staying. However, eight short-term hikers passed us and we calculated the lean-to would be crowded. Besides, they were carrying armfuls of beer which, in all probability, meant a late night of talking and laughing. All things considered, Gene chose a campsite near a quiet stream a short way down Tray Mountain Road. While he went looking for this site, I waited at the place where the Appalachian Trail crosses this dirt road. A battered car slowly approached and stopped. Two wizened, toothless hunters with their firearms resting between them asked me if I had seen any wild turkeys in my travels. Replying that Neel's Gap was the last place we sighted turkeys, I felt relieved when they drove off.

April 7

'A peaceful smile is expressed from the inside out.'

A week had passed since we first set out and we were feeling physically stronger each day.

Tray Mountain, a prominent peak of the Georgia Blue Ridge, afforded us excellent vistas and we lingered there admiring God's handiwork. It was great to be living in the house of the Lord!

After dinner, the warmth of the midday sun and a full stomach lulled Gene asleep as he leaned back against a tree, the empty pot still in his hand. I couldn't resist snapping this picture of contentment.

Going down to Addis Gap Shelter for water, we decided to remain and start out extra early the next day. Finding a secluded spot near the stream, I delighted in a complete sponge bath, being careful to discard my soapy water away from the stream. The collapsible basin our daughter, Mary, gave me worked well if it was filled near capacity, otherwise it folded in on itself.

I was beginning to feel much younger than my forty-seven years and concluded it was all the fresh air and exercise.

April 8

The heavy gray sky overhead and the dry leaves underfoot implied it was autumn, but the countless flowering pink and red bud trees, and occasional white sour apple trees, verified it was indeed spring. Climbing Kelly Knob began our day, which ended at Plumorchard Lean-to.

Late afternoon Gene left me resting by the trail with our packs while he went down to the lean-to to see if there was ample space for us. It seemed like he was gone a long time, but I was satisfied to be sitting on a rock.

Gene found only Howard in the lean-to and together, unbeknown to me, they cleaned up the entire area of all kinds of litter. They hid bottles, cans, broken lawn chairs and the remains of a charcoal grill in a nearby ditch before Gene came back to announce, "It looks great." A long time passed before he ever divulged the story of their spontaneous cleaning spree to make the area appealing to me. The close proximity of the paved road through Dicks Creek Gap, about four miles south, made this shelter readily accessible.

During the evening we learned Howard had hiked the entire Appalachian Trail several years earlier, but this time he was only going as far as Damascus, Virginia. Hearing him tell his story excited and inspired me.

April 9 North Carolina

During the night I heard rustling noises coming from behind the shelter. Knowing an animal was prowling, my heartbeat quickened and I strained to see in the darkness. Loud snorts startled me, as our presence alarmed the animals. However, the snorting did identify the animals, deer, and my body relaxed again.

Setting out at seven-thirty in the morning, a fine drizzle signaled us to put on our rain covers. These had been designed and sewed by Gene out of moss green, waterproof nylon material. Keeping the contents of our packs dry was of the utmost importance, like having a roof on one's house. As we rounded the side of the mountain, the rains commenced, scarcely giving us time to don our rain jackets. It wasn't long before our pant legs were soaked, the wetness slowly creeping up to our waistlines. Thick fog settled in making visibility about ten feet. Perspiring from exertion, we became completely soaked, warm moisture under our jackets and cold moisture on our legs.

Mid-morning we crossed the state line, leaving Georgia and the Catahoochie Mountains, entering North Carolina.

Here, Bly Gap was visually lost to us. A solitary tree, its trunk curved like a high-backed rocking chair, stood off to the right side, an inaudible invitation to be seated. Nevertheless, we trudged on and upward past Sharp Top. By the time we reached Court House Bald, the rains tapered off and we decided to break for lunch. Gene prepared our freeze-dried spaghetti dinner and tea, both hot and satisfying. We should have waited, though, as a half mile farther we discovered a new A-line shelter, not recorded in our guidebook. Howard, perched on the wide low shelf in the back, his wool cap set high on his head, resembled a smiling gnome. Although it was early, he easily convinced us to stay and get out of our wet boots and clothing. Then he quickly strung up his rain tarp across the back area, creating a private dressing room for me. His courtesy really impressed me!

Before long, seven more male hikers arrived and the shelter was filled to capacity. The wooden floor literally vanished under sleeping bags and equipment, all spread out, blending together. Watching all these men prepare their evening meal was interesting as each had something different to cook. One young man was experimenting with a tuna recipe, complete with herbs.

As I began to put my wet boots on to make a bathroom stop before retiring, Howard said, "Here, wear my dry sneakers to go outside." Lacing up his size twelve and a half sneakers, I grinned, not so much at how silly I looked, but how happy his thoughtfulness made me.

April 10

'A fire will warm my body but pleasant thoughts warm my spirit. I love you.'

On this balmy spring morning we walked through a grove of silver birch trees. Their bark was lustrous, resembling heavy satin, and invited touching. The landscape viewed from atop Standing Indian, the Grandstand of the Southern Appalachians, was extraordinary!

Nearby, on a grassy knoll, a cluster of daffodils swayed in the sunlight. The daffodils, so simple, formed such a striking contrast with the mountains, so splendid. A hawk gracefully glided in the open expanses. We stood there savoring the golden moment, hoping to etch it in our minds forever.

Our thirteen-mile day ended at Carter Gap Shelter, where we shared the warmth of a blazing fire and trail stories with Mr. Pearson, brothers Steve and Brett, and Howard. These men had also spent the previous night with us at Muskrat Shelter. This shelter was smaller and the brothers decided to set up their tent nearby. As was his custom, Howard read by candlelight before retiring. It was here, during the night, a mouse chewed holes in my best T-shirt.

April 11

'Together, it can be done! I love you.'

Today we passed the 100-mile mark, a milestone, and also encountered our first episode of rock climbing the last three-tenths mile going up Mt. Albert, also called "Big Albert." Hanging onto the rope Gene threw down to me, I pulled myself upwards, my boots gripping onto the rocks. Taking a glimpse backwards, a wave of nausea passed over me. The scenery was tremendous but to this novice, the perils took precedence.

At intervals throughout the day and the following weeks, a thumping sound, starting slowly and then accelerating, vibrated through the woods, disrupting the prevailing quiet. It was like hearing the earth's heart palpitate. To our astonishment, we later learned that this was the male grouse courting the female. The males beat their tail feathers on a hollow log creating this resonance. They also perform a kind of dance for the hen, over whom they fiercely fight each other.

In the evening as we were hiking down to Rock Gap Lean-to, we heard the flutelike call of the wood thrush. The song was hauntingly beautiful in the deep recess of the woods.

April 12

Eleven hours and sixteen miles after leaving Rock Gap Lean-to, we found the stone tower on Wyatt Bald. For awhile we thought we had missed the turn off, as it seemed farther than on the map and our muscles were beginning to rebel. Hiking on a minimum of food, a bowl of cereal for breakfast and rice with peas and carrots for lunch, this was indeed a very long but lovely day for us.

Walking along I touched the sprouting buds on the trees. The fine down on them felt similar to lanugo on a newborn baby. Seeing and feeling all this new life bursting forth uplifted me.

Howard welcomed us enthusiastically, "It was getting so late I didn't think you were going to make it tonight. I'm glad you did!" A large group of teenagers from Chicago had transformed the area into a tent city. The parapet of the tower proved to be an excellent vantage point for photographing the setting sun, an ever changing masterpiece of vivid colors.

We fell asleep listening to all the noise and laughter of these energetic young people.

April 13

"As long as our thoughts are positive, our day will always end with a smile."

Following a restless night, the consequence of twitching leg muscles, we left Wyatt Bald early in the morning. Our intention was to reach Wessor Creek Lean-to by nightfall. However, six miles later and one hundred yards past Cold Spring Lean-to, I had to stop. Completely devoid of energy and reserve power, I couldn't walk another step. Concerned, Gene spread out my space blanket in a sheltered area by a big rhododendron, arranging my mattress and sleeping bag on it. Collapsing upon it, I felt like I was on a floating cloud and drifted into a deep sleep. This was the climax of my first two weeks on the trail! Meanwhile, Gene rested and prepared our dinner. Following this interlude, I was able to go on.

Later in the afternoon, unaware of the recent reroute, we ended up hiking over an endless, giant-sized earthen roller coaster, all ups and downs, with a few sharp curves in between.

In the evening I became frightened on the edge of a rocky outcropping, which was at the beginning of a steep descent and stood there crying, feeling totally vulnerable, afraid to advance alone. After what seemed like a long time, Gene backtracked up to my position. Frustrated by my feelings of inadequacy and tired to the bone, I crossly remarked, "You think you're so smart because you can do anything!" He calmly replied with directions of where to put my feet and patiently guided me down.

Gradually darkness enveloped us. A bright moon shining through the bare trees and a beam from our flashlight vaguely illuminated the narrow path. At one point my light focused on a patch of white flowers, hepaticas, prompting a smile.

Nine-thirty at night, exhausted from the day's efforts, we set up our tent smack in the middle of the Appalachian Trail. Sleep came instantly.

April 14

Our spirits and bodies were buoyed by a solid sleep and a steaming cup of tea enabled us to hike down the mountain at a quick pace. After rounding two bends in the trail, we could see water off in the distance and then spied colors on several buildings, convincing us we were almost there. Much to our pleasure, the trail exited almost opposite the Nantahala Outdoor Center and restaurant.

To our surprise, a number of people who had passed us on the trail were in sight. Howard invited us to share his room in the motel, which had three double beds. The night before he had gotten into Wessor late and had to sleep on the floor because all the rooms were filled. He decided to spend another day to rest up and do chores.

Seated by a window in the restaurant, Gene and I looked out onto the Nantahala River and indulged in a scrumptious brunch of orange juice, coffee, quiche, salad, homemade bread and butter. Full stomachs made us feel fantastic! Finishing, we went next door into the outdoor shop and spent forty-eight dollars for food to sustain us while climbing the Stekoahs. Our first scheduled food drop was Fontana, thirty hard miles farther north! Seeing our bill, we agreed it was a good thing we had eaten first. Next, Gene volunteered to do our laundry at the outdoor washer and dryer, while I shampooed my hair and wrote letters.

In the early evening six of us gathered in the restaurant to share a family style dinner, listed as all you can eat, providing six people ate together. Howard, Chris, Steve, Brett, Gene and I happily devoured lima beans, peas with celery, cauliflower with cheese sauce, spinach salad, chicken, rice, and spice cake. Everyone relished every bite as well as the fellowship.

Later a storm centered overhead and the power went off. I wrote in my journal using a flashlight, thinking how nice it was to be indoors in a dry, warm bed, safe from the storm.

April 15

Weighed down with full packs and full stomachs, having partaken of a king-sized family style breakfast with the same hikers, we walked across the one lane bridge spanning the Nantahala River and a short way along the railroad tracks before the trail turned right to leave the gorge. I beamed as I looked skyward. A brilliant blue sky complemented these grand mountains.

Although the way was steep, I was bursting with energy and a sense of well-being. The Jump Up, a nearly perpendicular section, slowed us to a snail's pace. Badly eroded, it would have been a fiasco in rainy weather and we felt fortunate the sun was shining. Soon after we had a bird's-eye view of the beautiful gorge and river far below us and stopped to take pictures and rest.

Our climb continued steadily and Gene expressed feeling tired as he hadn't slept well during the night, probably due to eating too much supper. I unsuccessfully tried to persuade him to select a secluded spot where we could lie down together. The thought of loving one another in dazzling sunlight on these mountains excited me.

Howard reached Sassafras Lean-to long before we did and jumped out to get a candid picture of each of us as we came around the shelter. We chose to save Cheoah Bald for the following day and to spend the night here.

April 16

Our breakfast included "breaking bread" with Greg and Howard. The bread was a loaf of homemade onion bread carried out of town yesterday. Today, Holy Thursday, seemed to us the perfect time to share our special bread, complete with jelly, with our friends.

Again the trail went straight up and then straight down; there were no switchbacks here. The ups were strenuous miles and the downs equally stressful. No wonder this is called the High Country!

April 17 Good Friday

Although our tent faced East, anticipating sunrise, the sun never made an appearance. The dawn was overcast, and as soon as our tent and gear were stashed into our packs, the heavens opened up. Struggling uphill in the thunder and teeming rain, I contemplated Calvary and its meaning to me, and the woods felt sacred. At this point my thoughts turned to our son's funeral and the agony we experienced following his death. To stave off depression, I mentally relived our life with our two children — my mental energy gave me physical energy.

Fourteen miles later we reached Fontana Dam and hiked two and a half miles along a winding road to Fontana Village. Expecting a few shops, we found instead an area that resembled a sprawling estate. Feeling a bit strange hiking in, we located the information center and obtained directions. As Gene checked on vacancies in the lodge, I rushed to the Post Office and met four of our young friends there. The postal windows closed five minutes earlier. Brett told me to knock and, when I did, out came the postal lady. She smilingly agreed to sort out our mail. I was absolutely thrilled to be handed sixteen letters along with our package. The feeling of warmth and love that swept over me is unforgettable.

Entering our attractive room, the thought struck me at how quickly we passed from the spiritual richness of the woods to the material luxury of a posh lodge. After the woods, the large bathroom was ultra-modern and spotless. The brownish gold shower curtain was even decorated with a large bear! Did we laugh. On the alert in the woods, we never expected to find one in our bathroom.

Having shed our wet clothes for dry ones, we made the cafeteria our next stop. Heaping plates of salad and vegetables satisfied our craving for fresh foods.

We ended our day resting in bed between percale sheets with plump pillows arranged behind our backs, reading all our mail from family and friends.

April 18

On our way to breakfast we met Howard, all packed and hoping to leave. The park ranger was going to issue trail permits between nine and ten o'clock, and everyone, including through-hikers, needed one to hike through the Smoky Mountains. A small group of hikers gathered to wait for the ranger. I noticed a barefoot woman with long, curly hair, wearing an ankle-length skirt. Wondering whether someone appearing so pretty could be hiking the trail, I introduced myself. She told us her name was Jacque and, yes, she was indeed hiking the trail. In time, she and her friend, Syd, became friends of ours.

It turned out neither Howard nor we could get a permit for Saturday night, so instead, we invited Howard to share our room and sleep on the couch, a hide-away bed. His pleasure in being asked was apparent.

Consequently, a leisurely day was spent doing laundry, shopping, writing, talking and eating. During one of our long conversations, Howard commented that he didn't have any close personal friends. This surprised me as his warmth and friendliness had won me completely.

Before retiring, I requested the operator to call us at four in the morning so we could make the interdenominational sunrise services scheduled at Fontana Dam for six a.m. At ten p.m. the phone rang, the first time to hear a phone ring in almost three weeks, and a melodious voice informed us Father Gus would give us a ride to the dam if we were outside the lodge at five forty-five. We accepted this gracious unsolicited offer. Again, the Lord provided. Riding with Father, we knew we'd be on time.

April 19 Tennessee - North Carolina

"Knowing my home is at the end of my day should make my day much easier. I love you."

Accompanied by organ music, a group of about sixty people, gathered to worship together, sang "Jesus Christ Is Risen Today." As everyone read the 104th Psalm in unison, Gene nudged me and said, "Look!" The mist, which had completely obliterated the landscape minutes ago, lifted and revealed the mountains, God's gifts to us. White dogwoods bloomed nearby, adding to the beauty of this glorious Easter dawn. Our souls rejoiced.

When the service ended, we spoke with several couples and then bid farewell to Father Gus, whose jovial face was wreathed by a bushy beard.

As we crossed over Fontana Dam to enter the Great Smoky Mountain National Park, the sun appeared — a dazzling ball of light in the mist. For us it was like coming home! These were our beloved mountains, where many a weekend and vacation were spent hiking and learning them.

Five hours later, while we were lunching at Birch Springs Shelter, Howard came over the hill, waving his walking stick and calling out, "I thought I wasn't going to see you until next week." We, too, were glad to see him sooner than arranged.

Doe Knob was literally carpeted with spring beauties, delicate tiny blooms. Golden trout lilies with bowed heads were scattered in between and Gene laid on his stomach to photograph them to advantage. Bluets edged the trail going up to Mollie's Ridge and our assigned lean-to. It turned out to be a full house with much activity as a teacher with seven students and two weekend hikers arrived. With persistence and help from the weekenders, the young boys built a roaring campfire. However, a downpour promptly extinguished it, eliciting loud protests.

The day ended pleasantly as we lay in our bunks observing this group interacting with each other, learning the ways of the backpacker.

April 20

After sleeping twelve and a half hours, I awoke feeling great and remained in my sleeping bag, listening to the rain drumming on the roof. Here in the Smokies the average annual rainfall ranges from about eighty inches on the peaks to about fifty inches in the valleys, and one expects to get wet. The abundant rainfall helps account for the rich flora and fauna and the seven hundred miles of streams.

There was no hurry to get started as Spence Field Lean-to was our next stop and a short distance away. Howard stopped in on his way from Birch Springs to Russell Field. Even though dripping wet, he looked neat, like always. He told us several more people showed up at his shelter last evening and he had not been alone which pleased him and us. Later, as we passed Russell Field Lean-to we waved goodbye to Howard and did not realize this was the last time we would see our friend.

Spence Field Lean-to held a surprise — a group of seven more students and their chaperon teacher from Illinois, all trying to dry out. Scheduled to be at Derrick Knob today, they got doused by rain going up Thunderhead Mountain. Two of the teenagers had no raingear and their leader, Mrs. Shay, decided for safety's sake to backtrack. There were two empty bunks on the bottom tier and we quickly settled in. With that, the chain link door opened and in came six more teenagers and their teacher, wet, hungry and tired. They had been assigned to this place on this day. Grumbling, some of the others moved out and put up tents. Wet clothes, gear and steaming bodies were everywhere. Tempers improved considerably, though, as hot food was prepared and eaten.

It was still raining when the last candle was extinguished and the mice invaded. The mice marathon had begun!

April 21

Mrs. Shay's group left at five a.m., hoping to hike seventeen miles to their appointed stop. The second group arose leisurely and made blueberry pancakes. We felt relieved seeing everyone smiling, dry and eating with gusto.

Spence Field, a verdant mountaintop meadow, shimmered in the morning sunlight, its tall grass wet and lustrous. The trail, deeply eroded in places, wound two miles over a grass grown crest and up to Rocky Top, the second peak of Thunderhead Mountain. From this bald, the sweeping scene was outstanding, with Fontana Lake clearly visible.

Reaching Silas Bald Lean-to, we again found Mrs. Shay and her group, which did not surprise us at all. Only this time they were already camped outside the shelter.

April 22

A cold fog rolled in, erasing all the surrounding mountains and transforming the trees into vague images. Having travelled this path numerous times before, we knew what we were missing. By-passing Double Springs Lean-to, we shortly entered a spruce and balsam forest. Hushed silence filled this natural cathedral where life thrived, unseen but felt, all about us and we walked gently. The trill of a dark-eyed junco broke the silence, and we began talking in low voices. I asked Gene to pose for a picture here and it turned out to be one of my best photographs. Bracing one foot on a tree stump, Gene rested his hands on his walking stick and pensively gazed ahead.

The highest point in the Smokies, Clingman's Dome, is six thousand, six hundred forty-two feet high and attracts a steady stream of tourists to its observation tower. Although the visibility was poor, the flow of people never ceased. Resting on a stone wall, we watched them huffing and puffing as they reached the end of the half mile walkway leading from the parking area. It was unfortunate they would not see the hidden panorama, usually seen from the tower.

At Mount Collins, one of our favorite shelters in the Smokies, a family of four and a lone hiker greeted us. After talking briefly, we then got busy. Choosing upper bunks, we spread out our space blanket, mattresses and sleeping bags respectively, and then hung up our packs.

A huge fallen tree served as our supper table and work space, a nice convenience. Our tasks completed, we passed the evening conversing with these friendly people.

April 23

'The sun does not shine bright everyday. We need to experience a cloudy and rainy day to know when the sun is bright.'

Before leaving Mount Collins Shelter, the mother, Sandy, gave us two hi-protein drinks and two energy bars. This was the first time we accepted food from virtual strangers and it was a humbling experience. After the family put on their rain gear and packs, Gene took their picture to be sent with a thank you note after our return home.

We lunched at Ice Water Lean-to along with seven other hikers, all relieved to be under cover. The steady rain pounded the tin roof and water leaked in several places. Often the flow of conversation was broken with laughter. Our menu consisted of freeze-dried turkey tetrazzini and six M & Ms each for dessert. One of the day hikers observed me counting out the candy. He reached into his day pack and handed Gene two candy bars and two boxes of raisins, saying, "These are for you and your Mrs.; I think it is great what you two are doing." We were again touched by a stranger's kindness.

The next seven and a half miles of trail became a trial for me. The trail became a rivulet in places as the rain continued heavily. We had to stop for two bathroom stops. The first time I couldn't wait to go far off the trail but felt quite certain no one would come along. "After all," I reasoned, "there can't be too many people out in this kind of weather." How wrong I was! Squatting close to the earth, I saw legs go by. My privacy was invaded. Seeing that I felt mortified, Gene helped me to put things back into perspective by saying, "Well, I do declare!" This is what an elderly lady once uttered when she accidently caught him in the woods. We both laughed, although it was easier to laugh the time it was at his expense.

The last and sixteenth mile of the day was plain misery for me as I was feeling cold, tired and waterlogged. To make matters worse, my boots stretched from the wetness and my arches pained me. At long last, there was the Peck's Corner sign — one-half mile more, ALL DOWN.

The shelter was filled with people. Greg greeted us saying, "I have a cup of hot tomato soup ready for you. Get out your cups." This was a "peak" moment for me! The thoughtfulness of this young man warmed me even more than the soup he prepared us.

Gene held up our space blanket before me as I stood in the corner, a stone wall on one side and a wire grating, entwined with pine boughs, on the other side. In privacy, I peeled off all my wet clothes and pulled on my long-johns. Dry clothes, the comfort of dry clothes, was a daily occurrence never fully appreciated until now.

After Gene changed his clothing, we concentrated on fixing our supper of hot tea and more soup and crackers. Sitting opposite one another and gazing intently at each other, Gene took both my hands into his strong hands and kissed them. This simple, love-filled gesture made me feel beautiful.

Snug in my sleeping bag, warmth and contentment permeated my being. Maine, here we come!

April 24

We awoke with sunshine streaming in on our faces, what a wonderful gift for our anniversary.

Gene strung up a line between two trees so we could dry our clothes before leaving. With our next reservation only six miles away, there was ample time.

During the afternoon's walk, we stopped to rest and celebrate our day by eating as much gorp as desired. Along came John and Martina Linnehan, whom we had heard about and were anxious to meet. Following introductions and an explanation for our partying, John questioned, "Are you sure you two are married?" "You bet," replied Gene, "twenty-seven years!" Chilled from standing still, they said, "We'll see you at the shelter," and moved on.

Upon our arrival, all the people loudly chorused, "Happy Anniversary." To our intense pleasure Greg was there, too, and had a roaring fire going in the fireplace. John and Martina, who had never hiked before beginning their through-hike, regaled us with funny stories.

During the night the temperature dipped into the low teens.

April 25

'The pines do not drop their needles to shed the weight of snow. They smile throughout the seasons to bring us the joy we know. I love you.'

After leaving Tri Corner Shelter, a marvelous surprise awaited us atop the first hill. At this elevation the woods had been transformed into a crystal wonderland. Ice glazed all the stark trees, coating each slender branch and twig, magically capturing the morning sunlight. The coniferous trees drooped gracefully under the weight of their burden. In the distance the mountains glistened, their ragged edge, formed by tall spruce trees, jutted into the azure sky. We were deeply touched by the magnificence of our environment and our Creator's majesty. Gene turned around to me and said, "Today I keep thinking of Steve." I replied, "Steve's presence is real to me also. It is as though he is walking with us."

Our boots made crunching sounds as we trod along the frozen earth. Suddenly Gene stopped and became motionless. I walked from behind to look at him. Tears streamed down his rugged face. The pain and loss following Steve's death were still heavy upon us. There encircled by God's silent love, we stood together crying and shared silence.

April 26

We left Davenport Gap Shelter at ten a.m., now daylight savings time, after having spent a genial evening with John and Martina, John "the artist," and two couples out for the weekend. The warm day quickly became a hot day, and soon after crossing under Interstate 40, where we ascended a steep log stairway leading into the Pisgah National Forest, we changed into our shorts. Our legs were stark white compared to our tanned faces, arms and hands.

Blue periwinkles, scarlet Indian paint brushes, and yellow whorled loosestrife, early spring flowers, grew randomly alongside the trail going up Snowbird Mountain. These splashes of primary colors compelled us to stop, examine them closely and take pictures.

Soon the ideal lunch stop presented itself — a piece of level earth with a stream on either side, flowering dogwoods, violets and yellow daisies, all drenched in sunshine, with a faint breeze to cool us and a fallen tree to sit upon. Before sitting down to eat, Gene stuck his walking stick into the ground and screwed the camera onto the brass piece on top, creating a unipod. His handcrafted, specially designed, mahogany walking stick enabled him to take pictures of us together and, unexpectedly, turned out to be a conversation piece all the way to Maine.

Later, the West Peak of Snowbird afforded us three hundred sixty degrees of splendid views and shedding our packs, we literally ran around the low white fenced-in FAA installation building, wishing to see north, south, east and west.

Leaving there, a metal sign, posted on a tree, warned: "North Carolina, Wildlife, Bear Sanctuary." Gene said, "Stand by the sign, look scared and I'll take your picture." Remembering the time we faced an aggressive bear in the Smokies when we were on a weekend trip, I playfully complied. However, fresh bear dung noted on the trail farther along truly alerted me.

In the winter months the black bears hibernate in dens, only occasionally venturing forth on balmy days. During this period their digestive systems shut down and they do not eat, drink, urinate or defecate. With the advent of spring, the bears begin to roam but mainly live off their body fat gained the previous fall. Their meager diet consists of the leaves and stems of herb-like plants until the summer when they feast on blueberries, blackberries and raspberries, except for the small percentage that help themselves to hikers' food. I wondered, "Would a bear know our food reserves were sparse?"

Groundhog Creek Lean-to was different than the shelters in the Smokies. Firstly, it did not have wire fencing across the opened front to keep the bears out and, secondly, the interior had a raised, slanted wooden floor for sleeping. Greg

31

chose to sleep under the stars, thoughtfully making room for John and Martina, who arrived an hour or more after us.

For supper, we drank the high energy drink that Sandy had given us, using skim milk instead of water, and it helped to fill our empty stomachs. The others had hitched a ride into town and were eating real food.

Much to our disappointment, Howard never arrived as planned.

April 27

Knowing we only had a meager breakfast to prepare, we arose at five-thirty, hoping to leave before the others began cooking their bacon and pancakes. During the morning I could sense Gene's discouragement. Later, he revealed he was annoyed with himself, and with me, for not planning our food more wisely. He, too, was very hungry and grumpy. Approximately five miles into our day, we began our first road walking on Max Patch Road, a gravel road winding between picturesque farmlands. To our left three women hoed in the fields, as two elderly men sat close by watching them. A young child swung on the adjacent fence, playing.

I called to the nearest woman, inquiring if any of the farmers sold eggs. She in turn called to the other woman and asked her. "Yes, I have a dozen to sell!" Praise the Lord! We accompanied her back to the farmhouse across the road, paying her a dollar, although she only requested seventy cents. She said there were only eleven eggs but then went to the henhouse and brought back the twelfth egg, chicken feathers still clinging to it. To us the eggs were beautiful. Feeling our spirits rocket, we carefully placed the eggs in the top of my pack. Leaving, there was renewed spring in our steps.

We lunched beside a stream and joined hands to pray, as was our practice before eating. Again the Lord provided, just when we needed it most. Each of us ate two hard-boiled eggs. The jumbo eggs with their golden centers tasted better than any we had ever eaten.

Fortified, we hiked until six p.m., setting up camp on Bluff Mountain. Pink, peach and purple hues blended in the evening sky as I prepared custard for supper, using the last of our skim milk and four more eggs. Watching me carefully stir our supper to the perfect consistency, Gene praised my resourcefulness. Maslow's hierarchy of needs flashed into my mind and I smiled at my husband.

That night we went to bed feeling full. From this time on, whenever we reached a town, we bought and carried fresh eggs.

April 28

This morning we began our day with oatmeal without milk and four scrambled eggs. Nutrition-wise, we got off to a good start; weather-wise, it was warm and sunny, and we covered the thirteen miles to Hot Springs by four o'clock. Coming down off the mountain ridge, we could hear dogs barking, the sounds of moving traffic, and the high pitched voices of excited children. Stepping out of the woods, a large "Welcome Hikers" sign invited us to stop at the Jesuit Hostel, located here at the edge of town. Arranging to stay, I was assigned to the loft above the kitchen and Gene to a community room. Gene could later join me, though, as no other women hikers arrived. Next, Gene headed for the Post Office and I headed for the shower. On his way he stopped at a gas station and bought a Sprite and a bag of potato chips. Finishing them, he had another Sprite and another bag of chips. He returned, grinning, and carrying fourteen letters, a book from my sister and our package. We took our letters to the laundromat where, engrossed in reading them, the laundromat became tolerable. As happy as I was to wash our clothes, the laundromat usually depressed my spirit. Gene also treated each of us to a pint of ice cream.

Before returning to the hostel, we stopped at The Inn, an antiquated house that had been restored and was known for its natural home-cooked vegetarian meals, and made arrangements for breakfast. Jacque and Syd, John and Martina and John "the artist" were staying there overnight.

Back at the hostel, Greg prepared a spaghetti dinner and I fixed a big salad. Gene took several pictures of us working in the small kitchen where Greg made a unique chef in his shorts and baseball cap. Greg, Chuck, Gene and I sat outside at the picnic table to eat, downing heaping plates of spaghetti with sauce, salad, bread, butter and milk. I never ate so much before and yet, I did not feel too full.

A leisurely walk around Hot Springs, where the trail goes through the heart of town, completed our day. Eager to be present at the six o'clock church service the next morning, we crawled into our sleeping bags early, but quickly crawled out of them. The loft was hot; there was no cool night breeze here.

April 29

The early morning liturgy, held in the priest's living room, instead of the A-line chapel, was informal and special, and we received Communion in the form of bread and wine. I tasted and knew the Goodness of the Lord. At the conclusion of the religious celebration, Father invited us into his kitchen for conversation, juice and coffee.

Feeling we needed a day to rest our bodies, we decided to stay at the Alpine Motel the next night. The previous night's sleep was frequently interrupted by laughter and loud voices coming from the kitchen below us.

After a long nap, we went into town to shop and to enjoy a change of pace. Letters were written and our packs repacked with fresh supplies and laundered clothes.

An exceptional dinner at The Inn, where we joined John and Martina, completed our day off.

April 30

Before leaving town, we mailed a package home which contained my corduroy pants, down jacket and the set of Miller-Falls carving chisels we selected in the hardware store for Barry's birthday gift. Barry, a young man whom we love as a son, is the one who walked to the summit of Springer Mountain with us. There he celebrated the momentous occasion with us, praying with us and strongly embracing us farewell.

Our final purchase, a pint of ice cream each, was consumed sitting beside the French Broad River. The first three miles proved difficult, although the terrain was not. Our rhythm had been broken by staying in town and we had trouble gaining momentum.

At five miles we crossed the crest of extensive meadows on the south slope of wooded Mill Ridge. I took a picture of Gene coming over this parklike ridge, where white dogwoods blossomed and the grass hugged the earth like a plush green carpet. In the background could be seen the small pond that we had just circled. A boxed spring at the head of the pond fed this clean looking body of water. The next day we learned Jacque and Syd became ill from drinking water drawn from this spring. Gene refrained from taking water from here because of the openness of the area, having few trees and roots to filter the water, and the accessibility of the water to animals.

Later the winds in Hurricane Gap slowed me down even more. This gap earned its name! The last several miles before Spring Mountain Shelter were not fun; they merely tested my endurance. Spent, I had to push myself to keep walking. Finding John, Martina and Bill at the shelter, along with two others, laughter and camaraderie soon helped to dispel our tiredness. Peanut butter and honey sandwiches, along with hot chocolate, made our supper satisfying. Built to house five persons, six of us squeezed into this shelter constructed in 1938 by the Civilian Conservation Corps, while the seventh hiker slept in a string hammock. Fortunately, it did not rain.

May 1

The comforts of Hot Springs had indeed spoiled us and we hiked like there was lead in our boots even though the day began with a super breakfast. Our menu featured apple rings with cinnamon, prunes, wheatina, French toast and milk. At Allen Gap there was a gas station where ice cream could be purchased and our mid-morning snack consisted of a pint of ice cream each, despite the fact the day was cool. At first we thought we were out of luck as John had primed the clerk to call out, "Sorry, we just sold our last ice cream."

Even though we had covered twelve miles and were fatigued, the onset of rain convinced Gene we should push to reach Jerry's Cabin, three miles farther. The thought of sleeping inside a cabin motivated me but didn't speed me up and Gene kept turning around to see if I was still behind him. Later, Gene acknowledged this was the one and only time he felt impatient with my pace.

Sighting the structure, I realized my misconception. Jerry's Cabin was not a cabin; it was a shelter with a fireplace. What a disappointment this was. John's voice boomed encouragement, "Come on strong, Madelaine, you can make it!"

Filled to capacity, everyone was already in their sleeping bags. Bill, Paul, John and Martina, all through-hikers, moved over as far as they could. Two weekend hikers, heading south, took up space enough for four people as they had their packs on the sleeping platform and didn't offer to remove them. I felt as though we were intruding.

Working by the light cast by the fire crackling in the fireplace, where two chickens were roasting on a stick, Gene hung up our food, we stashed our gear and prepared hot chocolate for supper, considering it too late to fix anything else. John offered Gene a swig from his flask, which Gene gulped down. Whatever it was, it helped to soothe him.

Although packed in like sardines, we slept soundly. However, my psyche was crushed and I knew I needed to tent camp the next night.

May 2

The cold morning made it difficult to get out of our warm sleeping bags. John declared, "You don't get to Maine on a magic carpet!" Although we all smiled, we ignored his vocal prodding, and all of us got off to a late start.

Today I concluded a person cannot be well-fed and still carry a pack of sensible weight. It was an either or situation. Coming out of Hot Springs, I was laden down with fresh supplies and my pack weighed over forty pounds. Struggling uphill, I knew it was way too heavy for me.

Entering a small open area, we came upon the tombstones of William and David Shelton who fought for the Union Army during the Civil War. Buried in a common grave, their tombstones faced one another. Walking along, we verbally reflected upon the lives of these men and the pain and suffering they and their families must have endured.

Hiking out of Devil's Fork Gap was strenuous for me and we only covered about four miles before finding a suitable campsite just beyond a stream. Staggering at times, I mentally discarded unessentials from my pack, including butter, a candle and some clothes. In Hot Springs Martina had purchased a package containing two tubs of soft whipped butter and gave me one weighing four ounces. At the time I accepted it, it felt so light.

A spectacular supper was prepared to help eliminate some of my weight. Our meal consisted of instant mashed potatoes smothered in butter, green beans cooked in butter, tuna fish in chicken gravy using butter, crackers spread with thick butter, hot chocolate and M & Ms.

Before calling it a day, I propped my tiny oval mirror in the crotch of a tree to use and, no doubt, it is still there.

May 3

The way to Sam's Gap was long and Gene commented, "Today's climb was as steep as the Stekoahs but in one third the distance." However, the perfect weather, the farmlands and the high pastures made it an outstanding day. Besides, it was the Lord's day, which always made the woods feel extra special.

Mid-morning I sat facing the mountains, strung out beyond the rolling farmlands and briefly read from *Prayer Thoughts from the Psalms*, a booklet Pastor Gustafson's wife sent to me, and then meditated awhile.

Later, as we were finishing our dinner, a pot of rice pudding, I realized we were in the middle of a cow pasture. Looking all about me, I asked Gene, "Is that what I think it is?" Laughing heartily, Gene nodded affirmatively. Flat patties of cow dung were heaped all about us. Until this very moment the trees, mountains, food and Gene had monopolized my attention.

Farmers had built stiles of various designs enabling us to safely cross fences of barbed wire that separated one green field from another. Having climbed over a stile, we walked along a jeep road, edged by fruit trees. A four-wheel drive pulled up and the men called to us, asking if we'd like some cold beer. They were out to collect ramps and brought plenty of refreshment. We declined, saying we'd prefer ice cold water.

Big Bald, prominent to the northeast, stood out against the blue sky. Syd had encouraged us to camp there but we knew my limitations. Big Bald would have to wait. Instead, we set up our tent in a sag, away from the dirt roads.

Bathing, I was again astonished at the grime that came off. Most of the time we looked better than we smelled and felt better than we looked. This night, though, we crawled into our sleeping bags feeling clean and smelling sweet.

May 4

Standing on Big Bald in brilliant morning sunlight, I felt the goodness and graciousness of the Lord! Before us stretched the Southern Appalachians, Mount Mitchell in the Black Mountain Range, the Nantahalas in North Carolina, Mount LeConte in the Smokies and the Unakas to the northeast. The sight of all these peaks was edifying and filled me with emotion.

During the afternoon I fell, catching my boot in a root covered by leaves. My walking stick saved me from going head first and, instead, I landed on my derriere. Only my ego suffered.

About five o'clock we met Scott, set up and in the process of cooking his evening meal. His knees pained him, forcing him to stop early. Our knees were sore but, fortunately, not painful.

Leaving Spivey Gap, the last mile of the day took us up a steep ascent paralleling a rushing stream through birch, cherry, hemlock and rhododendron growth. On the top we found an irresistible site amid pine trees. Another extraordinary day ended as we lay in our sleeping bags, listening to an owl come closer and closer to our tent. The owl's repeated calls finally ended with an unusual gurgling sound.

May 5

From the narrow crest of Cliff Ridge we had excellent views of the Nolichucky River, the Clinchfield Railroad and several communities. The sounds of activity below gradually reached us and filled us with expectancy. Thinking of ice cream, we decided, upon reaching the bridge, to walk into Erwin and refuel. The two miles into town were pleasant ones; all the homes, gardens and lawns exhibited the owners' careful attention and pride.

While I waited in front of the supermarket with the packs, Gene was inside purchasing eleven dollars worth of groceries and two pints of ice cream. A delivery truck stopped near the newspaper dispenser, and the driver handed me a newspaper, telling me to catch up on the news. The paper not only kept me occupied but made a good fire starter. We carried the ice cream to a little park near the Baptist church and enjoyed it sitting at a picnic table.

For a mile we walked along the bank of the Nolichucky River and then noticed a kayak with the lettering, "Nolichucky Outdoor Center," suspended overhead between two trees. Persuading Gene to check it out with me, we had a refreshing surprise. For a dollar, I was able to have a luxurious hot shower and shampoo. Syd and Jacque were also there and Gene took two pictures of them while he waited.

Although camping areas were available for a fee, we decided to tent camp farther along the trail.

May 6

'It's good to lead but it's also good to know help is just behind me. I love you.'

Curly Maple Gap Shelter turned out to be an impromptu mid-morning gathering place for a group of us through-hikers. Eight of us — Chris, Brian, Syd, Jacque, Bill, Rodney, Gene and I — sat around snacking and caught up on trail news and happenings.

Farther along the trail Gene lost his footing on an eroded shoulder of the path and slid on his back down a bank and under some rhododendron bushes, where he became wedged. Flailing his arms and legs in an attempt to loosen himself, he resembled an inverted turtle. Close behind, I came to his rescue, trying hard not to laugh at his comical predicament.

Beauty Spot, a natural grassy bald known for its superb views, was adversely affected by the imminent rain. Presently, haze veiled Roan Mountain, the Blacks, Big Bald and Flattop Mountains and upper Toe River Valley. Syd and Jacque set up camp on the perimeter of the bald, hoping the dawn would break clear. We kept going, intending to prepare our dinner in Deep Gap but, instead, found ourselves climbing five thousand foot Unaka Mountain, before realizing we missed the meadow and water source described in our guidebook. Continuing to the summit, we finally had a supper of hard boiled eggs and raisin bread while standing in the shelter afforded by the tall evergreens. Although the area was flat and would make an excellent tent site, there was no water nearby. We decided to go on to Cherry Knob Shelter, three and one-half miles farther, arriving there near eight o'clock. Mike and Chris were already there and Brian soon joined us. Brian wore a miner's headlight to cook and get organized by, leaving his two hands free to work.

I wrote in my log by candlelight, burning the candle Syd had given me the day before, happy now to have carried this luxury item—a candle.

May 7

A fine drizzle fell, making the woods damp. All the wild flowers bowed their heads to receive this tender blessing. A straggly brown dog appeared from beneath the undergrowth and followed us to the Clyde Smith Shelter, where we found Mike napping. Hearing us, he aroused, and we three chatted as Gene and I prepared our hot meal. Before long other hikers appeared and the shelter filled up. Learning I had left my mirror behind, Bill Fisher offered me his mirror, saying he no longer had a need for it. His bearded face verified this.

After eating and reading the guidebook on the terrain, we decided to wait until morning to start out. Stiffness was settling in my joints from all the dampness and, besides, it was fun being amongst all these people. "Lightfoot," named such because his pack weighed only twenty-two pounds, whistled as he prepared his soup of wild ramps.

By evening time five tents could be seen clustered about the shelter area with everyone hoping for a clear day to climb Roan Mountain and the Highlands of Roan.

May 8

'This is a beautiful world when I make it so. I love you.'

41

I awoke during the night feeling cold. Peering out of my sleeping bag, I noted the clouds had dissipated and stars filled the sky. I aroused Gene to tell him the good news, "The stars are shining!" Within myself, I whispered, "Praise the Lord!"

The way was steep and it took us until one-thirty to reach the top of Roan Mountain. A paved road and the trail converged here in a park area complete with a picnic table and restrooms but there were no other people. Pine trees abounded everywhere.

On Roan High Bluff we lunched in a small clearing in front of a rustic log cabin. As we were relaxing, Paul, a young man of college age and also a through-hiker, arrived carrying his recently purchased guitar strapped to his backpack. Sitting by the log cabin, he strummed softly, creating a picture of contentment. I closed my eyes and heard our son playing his guitar.

By three-thirty we began traversing a chain of bald mountains. Since it was a perfectly clear day, we could see in all directions. At six we came to a newly constructed lean-to and found Bill by himself. We decided against stopping as we wished to arrive in Elk Park the next day in time for our mail drop before the post Office closed at ten-thirty. After crossing several stiles and grazing lands, we were back on the balds.

The day was ending all too quickly. It was dramatic racing across Yellow Bald at sunset. The winds were forceful and stung our legs as we still had shorts on. I kept glancing to my far left to watch the setting sun and marvelled at the bands of color — rose, red and magenta — sweeping across the evening sky. Seeing my giant-sized shadow running beside me gave me a strange feeling. Small me could cast such a big shadow! As I hurried behind Gene I kept thinking about the impact one person can make in this world.

Descending into a shallow gap, dotted with trees, we hurriedly put on all the clothes we carried in our packs, erected our tent and crawled into it. For supper we ate sticky peanut butter on crumbling saltines and drank reconstituted gatorade. Keeping everything on, we struggled into our zipped-together sleeping bags. The Lord gave us green pastures, a cow pasture, and we were not only surrounded by trees but by dried dung. I will remember this day forever! Feeling secure, satisfied and silly, we fell asleep laughing.

May 9

We awoke at six a.m. and had a sparse breakfast of honey and tang before leaving Bradley Gap and ascending the main slope of Hump Mountain, 5,587 feet high. Out in the vast openness, the winds once again buffeted us and, at times, actually took our breath away. This morning, however, we had on all the clothes we carried, making a decided difference, and pressed ourselves into the wind and dense fog. Glancing downward, we saw a trail of cattle prints in the mud. Imagine a herd of cattle crossing this heath bald. What a spectacular sight they'd make!

The sun sporadically broke through as the mist began swirling around. Soon the edges of mountains began to appear off in the distance, while little windows opened up in the mist, giving us glimpses of villages in the valley far below. As they'd close, others would open. Thrilled, we stood still, feeling very much a part of this theatrical dawn on Big Hump.

We arrived on the outskirts of Elk Park at ten-fifteen, where Gene left me with the packs in front of a grocery store and literally ran the mile to the Post Office, no easy feat in heavy hiking boots. Arriving a minute before closing time, he met John and Martina coming out, carrying our mail, but no package. While Gene was gone, I called my parents and had a wonderful visit.

Walking into town, we stopped in the Country Restaurant and had a king-sized breakfast of eggs, bacon, pancakes, coffee and biscuits. By the time we got to the motel, John had already reserved us a room and the owner volunteered to do our laundry as there was no laundromat in town.

A long hot bath, during which time I read all our mail, produced a clean me. Then Gene showered and we headed down Main Street to locate a barber shop, where Gene had his hair cut and beard and mustache trimmed. Groomed, my partner looked very handsome. Our purchases consisted of a small teflon frying pan, a bottle of white wine, cheese, crackers and fruit.

Before retiring, we talked to Gene's sister in Michigan and to his mother in Florida, but were unable to reach our daughter in Birmingham, Alabama, or Barry in Tennessee. At this time, Barry was the one sending out our pre-packed packages from home. Gene felt annoyed that our package had not arrived in time, as it meant staying over Sunday in hopes it would arrive on Monday.

May 10

Sunday, a damp rainy day, was spent writing eleven letters and postal cards, making phone calls and resting. Jacque and Syd stopped by our room to bid us farewell, as they were leaving the trail earlier than planned. Syd's mother drove to Elk Park to pick them up, and we went out to the car to meet her and to give them a final hug.

We finally reached our daughter, Mary, by phone at nine-thirty. Mary sounded dejected and lonely as she was on the verge of severing a close relationship with someone she deeply cared for. Our hearts were heavy as we went back to our motel room and we seriously considered taking a Trailways Bus to Birmingham. Could we possibly make things easier for our daughter and make her pain less? Talking out our feelings, Gene summarized it by saying it'd be like applying a bandaid on a deep wound. It must heal slowly, from the inside out. We must trust the Lord to care for our Mary, as only He could satisfy all her needs.

May 11

Our package arrived, verification we should continue on the trail. It turned out our box had been mailed on the specified date, allowing two weeks for delivery, but came via a very circuitous route. From this point on Gene decided to have our packages sent by priority mail.

Happy to be returning to the trail even in the rain, we repacked and headed out of town. Along the way, Gene found a three piece aluminum knife, fork and soup spoon, all snapped together, and considering its usefulness, he stuck it into his pack to become part of our standard equipment.

May 12

Freshly exposed rhododendron roots belonging to bushes cast to the side, and loosely packed dirt were evidences this section was a recent reroute. As we ascended a gradual incline, faint barking could be heard, coming from various directions. Quickly the barking increased in fervor and pitch and sounded like it was coming from one direction, behind me. I turned around to find a pack of at least seven dogs charging up the trail after me. They were every size, shape and color. I screamed for Gene who, fortunately, was only about ten feet ahead. Gene yelled, "Put out your stick!" Instead, I ran past him, my heart thumping wildly. Gene moved swiftly and brandished his heavier walking stick, poking the snarling lead dog in the shoulder. The animal stopped in his tracks and the rest of the yelping menagerie followed suit and soon dispersed. All afternoon I imagined I could hear dogs barking and stayed close upon Gene's heels.

Moreland Gap Shelter was empty when we arrived about five-thirty and we settled in. I found Don Farrell's address affixed to a newspaper heading, called the "Cape Codder," hanging in the lean-to and put it into my pack. We didn't know if or when we would see him again.

After awhile three young men from Allen, Pennsylvania, appeared. Ricky, Mickey and Tim made our evening come alive with laughter and music. This was Rick's first trip away from home and his parents agreed that this experience would be good preparation for college. However, his mother helped pack his backpack before he left on his trip and made up the packages she sent to him. Rearranging the contents of his

45

pack, he first took out three bars of unopened soap. Every time his mother sent a package, she sent another bar of soap. He hadn't washed his eating utensils in three days, much less himself! Secondly, out came an economy size toothpaste, unsqueezed. Next came a five pound bag of candy snacks, which he would have gladly traded for powdered milk. He yearned for cold milk. The other two teased him good naturedly each time he extracted something.

Mickey fixed chocolate pudding for the three of them, taking it down to the stream to chill it. He didn't particularly care for pudding at this time but wanted to lighten his pack.

The day ended with Tim playing his guitar by the campfire.

May 13

'A moment's rest, when rest is needed, will help us to experience the day with enjoyment.'

Descending into a gorge, we encountered the only rocky section all morning and we carefully worked our way down to the foot of Laurel Falls. Deep in this chasm, glancing skyward, we were struck by the powerful force and beauty of these life-giving tumbling waters. We spontaneously clapped and yelled, "Yeah, God!", like we did at the close of our Marriage Encounter Weekend. Tarrying, we had our dinner while listening to nature's symphony.

The trail paralleled Laurel Fork, crystal clear in the afternoon sunlight. It was a sportsman's dream and we recognized Matt, another through-hiker, sitting on a rock in the middle of the stream, fishing.

About four o'clock, we took a sharp right turn and began the extremely steep ascent out of the gorge to the top of Pond Mountain, where we selected a campsite, but only after Gene scouted a water source. To capture the precious water, detected trickling out of the dirt bank, he constructed a small reservoir out of stones and lined it with moss peeled from nearby trees and rocks. The weight of additional rocks kept the natural mortar in place. This ingenious engineering feat took time and patience but resulted in a pool of fresh cold water, continually fed by the seeping spring.

While waiting for Gene to return, I got into my long johns, readied the food bag to hoist up for the night, arranged our sleeping bags, and then read from the Psalms. I had the feeling we were alone on this mountain — a special feeling and a special place for us.

May 14

Dawn was warm and delightful, the beginning of another sunny day. Without details on this relocation, we had to estimate our progress. It was near noontime and about five miles into our hike, when we came onto Highway 321. An unexpected small store became our dinner place, where sitting in a booth, we feasted on cheeseburgers, french fries, milkshakes and double dip ice cream cones.

The afternoon was spent hiking around Watauga Lake and across Watauga Dam, erected by TVA between 1942-1949, as a unit of its multi-purpose system of dams. Pink lady slippers blossomed in this area and Gene took the necessary time to expertly photograph them. All the while, a cool breeze came off the lake, keeping us comfortable.

Vanderventer Shelter was perched on a rocky bluff, high above Watauga Lake but, luckily, the front opening did not face the water and wind. In the middle of the night, we were rudely awakened by an electrical storm—thunder, lightning, rain and hail. I cuddled closer to Gene, remembering the people who had been struck and killed by lightning last year at Double Springs Lean-to in the Great Smoky Mountains.

May 15

Gene served me coffee and breakfast in my sleeping bag, as I leaned against the wall of the shelter, my air mattress wedged behind me. Misty and drizzly, the morning did not warrant jumping up. We thought about our daughter, Mary, as this was the day of her candlelight ceremony prior to her graduation tomorrow. Mary was going to give her testimony and we prayed the Lord filled her with joy and calm on this important evening in her life, and that she would always sing the Lord's praises and be filled with His love.

Getting underway by nine o'clock, we found the trail soft and gently sloping for the ensuing fifteen miles. The trail passed an old brick chimney, standing desolate in a clearing. A cracked tombstone, set into the chimney read:

"Uncle
Nick Grindstaff
Born
Dec. 26, 1851
Died
July 22, 1923

Lived alone, suffered alone
and died alone."

Walking along behind Gene, I thanked God for my husband — my lover, my best friend, my partner. I was thankful I was not alone.

May 16 Virginia

An aching left hip awakened me. Heavy fog had settled in and it was raw and cold. Gene didn't appear to be in any hurry to budge and I decided to reverse things and give him the royal treatment this morning. As he was being served breakfast in his sleeping bag, through-hikers Fred and Bill (also brothers), arrived. They commented on how Gene had it made and in reply Gene simply grinned like a cheshire cat. Little did they know the opposite was true.

As our feet walked the trail, our hearts were in Birmingham, Alabama. About the time Mary was to be awarded her diploma, we applauded in the woods, smiling and crying together. We reminisced about her graduation from kindergarten, grammar school, high school and nursing school. Missing this graduation was one of the sacrifices necessary to hike the trail this year.

Eighteen miles and twelve hours later, we walked into Damascus, reputed as the friendliest town along the trail. The driver of a car stopped to direct us to the hostel. After purchasing groceries, we headed to "The Place," an old house provided by the Methodist Church. It was unfurnished except for a large picnic table with benches, an old couch and some foam mats in the upstairs bedrooms. Going from room to room, we found about twenty-six hikers, many of whom we had previously met. Since it was literally a full house, we spread out our sleeping bags in the corner of the living room, and visited awhile before turning in. I fell asleep half listening to a lively group discussion taking place in the kitchen; the topic centered on the advantages of taking the old Iron Mountain Trail versus the Appalachian Trail.

May 17

The mass exodus of hikers from "The Place" awakened us as their heavy boots clumped about overhead and down the stairs, shaking the floors, echoing throughout the house.

As we ate breakfast on the back porch, the postmaster stopped by and invited everyone to the eleven o'clock Methodist service. As much as I wanted to go, I couldn't bring myself to go in my hiking shorts. My long pants were filthy and stuffed in the laundry bag ready to go to the washateria. The neighboring Baptist Church piped organ music over a public address system and the strands of Amazing Grace filled the damp air.

Later in the day the postmaster returned and offered to take the hikers to the Post Office in his "pony express," a pickup truck, to collect their mail. Imagine having the Post Office opened on Sunday! The biggest surprise, though, was receiving a package from Howard containing his silk water carrier, facts sheet, homemade cookies, granola bars and envelopes of gatorade and lemonade. He also enclosed a letter explaining that he had left the trail due to depression and loneliness, triggered by all the rain. Included was a copy of the story about the six year old boy who hiked the trail with his parents. This was a "peak moment" for us.

We shared some of our cookies with those gathered around the table. Before long, the conversation turned to the Iron Mountain Trail, in existence since 1972, versus the present Appalachian Trail, which is thirty miles longer. What puzzled me was why so many hikers made such an issue over it. I intended to go over the present Appalachian Trail, even though longer. For myself, hiking the trail was more than making miles. Listening, though, I learned something very important. Everyone is on the trail for a different reason and their reason influences how they hike the trail. Everyone's hike is unique and is as individual as they are individual.

May 18

Damascus boasts an expert cobbler, C. R. Stout, and he skillfully nailed and reinforced the soles on Gene's boots while Gene sat waiting in the City Shoe Shop and Shoe Store. Earlier, Gene had tried using Crazy Glue, obtained in Fontana Village.

Next, Gene purchased a much needed pair of pants. Wearing a size thirty-six going into the men's shop, he came out sporting a trim thirty-two, and a broad smile and a justly inflated ego. It was over twenty years since Gene could wear a size thirty-two trouser! While Gene stopped in the hardware store to buy a piece of PVC pipe, I couldn't resist going into Adam and Eve's. All the pretty clothes tempted me to try on a sundress. My reflection in the mirror said, "Feminine but impractical, too loose in the waist and far out with hiking boots." Satisfied, I hung the dress back on the rack and, instead, selected an organdy and lace blouse to send home to Mary. The Post Office was our last stop before reluctantly leaving this outstanding little town.

Nine miles of hiking rounded out our day.

May 19

It rained all night and we had to pack up in the rain. A wet tent fly added considerable weight to Gene's pack. However, the aluminum poles went into my pack and their weight remained constant. Because of the weather, we opted to eat a cold breakfast and not lose any more time.

During the course of our day, we discovered a large turtle, numerous firepinks and a baby calf, not more than several days old. The skies cleared temporarily but then the rain resumed.

This was the first time we set up camp in heavy rains, quite a feat. Gene planned our strategy; every move was anticipated. And it worked! By erecting the tent fly first, instead of last, we were able to keep the tent proper dry. I even got a kiss as we huddled under the space blanket to remove the tent and poles from the bag. This was also the first time Gene didn't hang the food bag and I prayed the mice and wildlife would decide it was too wet out to hunt food.

May 20

'The Appalachian Trail took me through all kinds of weather, and so does life. I love you.!'

Pounding rain awakened us and we decided to wait awhile to see if it would subside. Time passed quickly as we talked and loved one another.

Gene decided a hot breakfast was in order to brave the elements. Using our space blanket, he rigged a fly over our entrance and cooked wheatina, bacon and eggs, fruit and coffee, thus fortifying us for what was in store. After repacking under the fly, we grudgingly put on our clammy clothes. The rain stopped just as we were about to take down the tent and the interior remained dry.

Hiking up White Top, I slipped on a rock and my right leg went under me. However, I experienced no immediate effects. Coming over the summit, which was wide open, Gene called, "It's a good thing it isn't raining!" With these words uttered, the rains returned, blowing horizontally into our faces. We carefully watched for the AT blazes painted on rocks and sticks, as there were no trees, and were glad when they led us back into the woods, which afforded some protection.

Finding Deep Gap Shelter empty, we quickly changed out of our wet clothing. I crawled into my sleeping bag to warm up while Gene prepared steaming hot coffee, which we enjoyed with the cookies Howard had sent us. It was a pleasure to read the register, particularly the remarks our trail friends had written.

Early evening another older hiker arrived and Gene helped him unzip his wet clothing as his hands were numb and non-functioning. Then he served him a hot cup of coffee in his sleeping bag.

The three of us talked and one by one feel asleep.

May 21

'Only our legs can take us to places where our mind can absorb the beauty of His creation. I love you.'

A clear, cold dawn and the joy of observing deer grazing near the shelter began our day.

In order to reach the peak of Mount Rogers, we had to detour off the Appalachian Trail but this is one place we were anxious to see. The Fraser fir and red spruce trees, filling the air with their unique fragrance, were so dense we could not see anything but the trees. Only a wooden marker convinced us we had, indeed, reached the top.

Later in the morning, we paused at Rhododendron Gap to take a picture of Gene standing high on a huge boulder, pensively surveying the surrounding six thousand acres of green mountain meadows. At this point we chose to take the new longer reroute through Grayson Highlands State Park and walked eight miles in a remote alpine setting where sheep grazed and black angus cows, ponies and horses roamed freely. We basked in the warmth of the sunshine, the peaceful atmosphere and the natural beauty of this place. The only sounds were those of the light wind and occasional locust.

All around us was space, wide open space. An acute awareness of space swept over me and I knew total freedom.

Our day ended trekking over Pine Mountain with aching feet to camp at Orchard Knob Shelter. We faced Mount Rogers and the setting sun!

May 22

This was another gorgeous day and we hiked ten and one-half miles, arriving at Dickey Gap shortly after noontime. We agreed to walk two and a half miles farther to Racoon Shelter, where there would be a reliable source of water for cooking and a shampoo.

Restored, we delighted in hiking into early evening, at which time we crossed a pasture where cows grazed in the fading sunlight. This peaceful scene soothed me and, although my body was tired, my soul was refreshed.

At seventeen miles my feet gave out and I abruptly announced that I couldn't go another step. Looking distressed, Gene persuaded me to keep walking, as the rocky area resisted being a suitable tent site. About a mile farther, we came to a tiny patch covered by high weeds. Instinctively we knew this was our place and stopped. Once settled in, Gene requested that next time I give him some advance warning as it disturbed him to push me to exhaustion but he had had no choice. From this point on, I'd tell Gene when my strength was ebbing and he'd learn to better read my face.

May 23

The headquarters for the Mount Rogers National Park turned out to be an outstanding stop and a source of information on the history and geography of the area, wildlife and flowers. At Gene's request, the helpful ranger posed in front of the wall mural that vividly captured the essence of the pastoral area we had been hiking in. Only after petting the stuffed bobcat and rearranging its placement to be certain it'd be in the picture, did I see the sign, "Please do not touch."

Gene left me there to browse and read while he walked several miles downhill to a small store. Obtaining a ride back, he brought a gallon of ice cream with him, which we shared with Sandy and Neil before getting underway again. However, the ice cream didn't tide us over very well and we stopped to eat peanut butter and honey sandwiches.

Coming down the mountain we heard strains of music, as clear as a bell on a cold winter's night. Our steps quickened to the rhythm. What a surprise to hear real music in the mountains, being accustomed to only hearing nature's music, the sound of the air and the whisperings of the trees.

In a clearing we found a young woman sitting on a stump, playing a banjo, while her husband and another couple sat nearby listening. We briefly visited with them before starting up Glade Mountain.

At seven-thirty, choosing a flat campsite on top, we put up our tent, and Gene backtracked to a source of water noted on the way up. Our PVC pipe and silk water carrier enabled him to collect and carry a good supply of water. There was even enough to bathe with, guaranteeing me to rest better and to feel well cared for. Gene recently remarked, "I feel good when I make you comfortable." And he's doing just that, spoiling me, as always. "Virginia is for lovers." That's us.

May 24

An occasional glance behind will help me stay on course. I love you.

Following a leisurely three course Sunday breakfast, we breezed along until Gene had to make a bathroom stop. Taking the camera, I kept going and, wishing to surprise Gene with the distance covered, moved along at a fast pace, even successfully crossing a brook without getting my boots wet. A divided path presented itself, with the less used one continuing as the AT.

I felt frisky being in the lead and clambered over a fence with only moderate difficulty. Something at this point told me to wait. Perched on the top rail of the fence, I waited and waited. A half hour passed before Gene appeared, scowling and obviously angry.

As Gene vented his feelings, I learned he did not want me to get too far ahead and thought I had taken the wrong path when he didn't easily catch up with me. Backtracking, he took the other path and met three men, who replied they had not seen a female hiker. Anxious, he again retraced his steps, running in places, shouting to me, without benefit of a reply. Having Gene angry with me, a rare happening, upset me and marred our morning. Three miles of road walking and discussion restored his smile.

Passing the Valley Restaurant, we splurged on a full course steak dinner with cherry cobbler and ice cream for dessert. Our packs had to be left outside and everyone who came in, dressed in their Sunday best, scanned the room. In our attire, there was no doubt to whom they belonged. When leaving, the waitress kindly sold us fifteen homemade rolls.

Passing a phone booth, we called Staten Island, eager to learn if our daughter had safely arrived at my parents', where she was planning on spending a week. She had, and was presently off to New York City with my sister, Teddy, to visit the Metropolitan Museum of Art. Also, my father loved to have us check in periodically so he could plot our progress and know our whereabouts.

Crossing under Interstate 81, the trail meandered through farmlands, where a farmer offered us a ride in a wagon, carrying children, and pulled by a John Deer tractor. Declining, we thanked him, explaining what our intent was.

At Crawfish Gap we discovered a thoughtful hiker had left a detailed written description of the new twenty-three mile reroute in a ziplock bag attached to the signpost. This kindness permitted us to copy all the instructions not in our old Virginia guidebook. Heading up the reroute, we passed a spring but Gene preferred to go back for water once we found a campsite. It turned out he had to repeat a mile each way.

May 25

A herd of cows, gathered under the trees, was startled by our approach and stampeded downhill ahead of us. Their cumbersome bodies crashed through the woods, leaving clouds of dust behind.

Walking along Route 42 in Ciras, we stopped to chat with a couple working in their vegetable garden. The next thing we knew, we were in their kitchen being served freshly brewed coffee, toast with real butter and homemade strawberry preserves. The Haytons, celebrating their twenty-fourth wedding anniversary on this day, made us feel as though they had awaited our arrival.

Late in the afternoon, we found a farm pond on a ridge, resembling a grassy meadow and boasting various kinds of fruit trees. Although it had all the requisites of the perfect campsite, the clouds looked threatening. We didn't want to get caught here in a storm, as the markings were sparse and difficult to find under the best conditions.

Passing over Chestnut Knob, we hiked about another mile before finding a flat spot large enough to set up for the night. Our chosen place overlooked a tranquil valley. A rim of mountains framed this green oasis, known as Burke's Garden.

Exhausted, I crawled into the tent and was asleep before Gene finished the night chores.

May 26

Five and a half miles without water and with none in sight left us feeling parched. It was providential that we met Sandy and Neil, who thoughtfully gave us each a drink of their water.

Miles later, Gene heard water running under the rocks beneath our feet. Halting, within seconds, he thrust his PVC pipe (bought for this purpose) between the rocks and worked it around until clear, precious water flowed out the other end; a faucet had been turned on. Each of us gulped down two cups and then slowly drank several more, relishing its wetness and coldness. Our thirst quenched, we printed a note, put it in a plastic baggie and hung it on a tree, indicating the source of water for all other hikers and to warn southbound hikers there was no more water until the pond, almost ten miles away.

That evening we set up our tent on a slope of Brushy Mountain. The rains came!

May 27

It rained all night and was still raining heavily as we broke camp. Sloshing down the trail, we spotted Sandy and Neil's Bivac tent set up in the middle of the trail. Approaching, we could hear their laughter, triggered by our loud splashing and Gene's absurd question, "Are you nice and dry?"

By the time we reached Interstate 77, we were drenched. We had to scale a guardrail and carefully work our way down a slick grassy slope, as here the trail crossed over the highway. Walking alongside the roadway, the cars and semi-trucks zoomed past us, creating suction that made us brace ourselves each time one passed. After the quiet of the woods, their speed, exhaust and noise bombarded our nervous systems. I thought, "God, this is ludicrous." My foot pained me but the transition back into civilization was even worse.

On the verge of tears, I saw a green sign in the distance, but without benefit of my glasses and with the rain, it was blurry. Finally, the wording, "Bland - 1 Mile," came into focus. "Lord," I prayed, "help me to make it." We had been hiking along the highway over an hour, but it seemed an eternity. By the time we reached the gas station, all the truckers had informed the attendant, via CB radio, two hikers were on their way into town. He greeted us, "You sure made good time!"

Bland had a motel, and although very small, it had a vacancy. Going to our room, we recognized Sandy and Neil's packs standing outside another door. How did they manage to get there first?

Later, we learned that the new Virginia guidebook detailed a shortcut into Bland, avoiding the highway. Carrying an outdated Virginia guidebook caused us much anxiety through the entire state.

That evening we were able to reach Mary by phone and arranged for her to meet us the following day on her way home from New York to Tennessee. Waiting for her arrival would give me a chance to rest my swollen foot, and hopefully heal it. Knowing our daughter was coming filled us with joy; we had so much to share with each other, so much to talk about.

May 28

Knowing rest was the best treatment for my foot, my day was spent in bed, catching up on letter writing. The rain never ceased and flash flood warnings were issued, making it easier to stay inside. Hearing of my problem, Sandy stopped by to visit awhile.

Matt and Bob, through-hikers, arrived in town, drenched and shaken by their frightening experience when Bob almost drowned in a fast moving, swollen river that had been a stream the previous day.

Learning there was a laundromat in Bland, Gene gathered together all our soiled clothes, only to return several hours later, looking sheepish and giving a detailed account of his experience. Beginning to retrieve the clothes from the dryer, he pulled out a tiny blue long sleeved shirt. Thinking he was in the wrong dryer, embarrassed, he quickly tossed it back in and slammed the door shut. Trying to appear nonchalant, he casually walked up and down, "eye-balling" each dryer for some familiar item. After several unsuccessful checks, the knowledge dawned that he had indeed opened the correct dryer. That little blue shirt was, in reality, my expensive Damart Thermolactyl undershirt, shrunken to a child's size by the heat. The bottoms were now about a foot long. Although the instructions on the label advise to avoid heat of any kind and to drip dry, Gene had forgotten. This costly mistake lightened my pack by twelve ounces, but the thought of all the cold, rainy days ahead without my longies made me shudder.

At last, about seven in the evening, there was loud knocking on our door. Gene jumped up from his twilight sleep and flung open the door to greet our daughter, Mary, who seeing her father for the first time with a beard and mustache, and thirty pounds lighter, burst into uncontrollable laughter. There they stood, hugging and laughing — a memorable reunion. Mary was a picture of loveliness and I was thrilled by her very presence.

Late that night, Gene got into his sleeping bag, spread out on the floor, and Mary and I shared the double bed, talking into the wee hours of the morning.

May 29

Conversation monopolized our day and it slipped by all too quickly. Standing in front of the general store's gas pump, the mannequin "weather-girl" shed her bright yellow raincoat and proudly modelled her bikini, indicating fair weather. If the forecast called for rain, she sported the slicker, like she had since we arrived in town. With clearing skies, we drove back to the trail to show Mary where we hiked from to meet her and walked a little way on the trail together.

Our next stop was the Western Sizzler on Interstate 81, where Mary treated us to dinner. Mary's car had momentarily changed the meaning of miles.

Late in the evening, Gene answered the loud knock on our motel door. A tall, dark-haired, intense looking man introduced himself as Rob Weisser, a through-hiker from New York. After brief preliminary talk, he asked who wrote our entries in the registers found in the lean-tos. Learning that I wrote our comments, Rob expressed his feelings of anger stimulated by my words written in the notebook left by Scott in Vanderventer Shelter. The way Rob read my words, he felt I was writing in anger. This completely floored me as never once did I feel anger since being on the trail — only a deep peacefulness. I tried to recall word for word what I had written. The gist of my entry stated we were hiking the 1981 trail (underlined to accentuate the importance to me), meaning taking all the reroutes and no shortcuts. It was imperative to me to hike the trail in this manner, as I waited a long time for this opportunity and I wished to experience it all. Several times Scott had given us unsolicited directions for alternate routes, and knowing the book would ultimately be sent back to him I questioned his reason for doing this.

It really distressed me that I had unwittingly aroused feelings of anger in a person I had never even met. We three expressed our feelings and I clarified what was intended in my written word. Back in Damascus, it became clear to me each person must hike the trail in his own way, for his own reasons, in his own time. I admired Rob for being so straightforward and open and in seeking me out and giving me the opportunity to explain myself.

This night I learned two important lessons. First of all, it would have been best for me to ask Scott, in person, why he was telling people of alternate routes. Secondly, the written word carries a tremendous risk. In writing my feelings I am making myself totally vulnerable.

Before Rob left, he told us about Lisa and Pete, trail friends of his, who would be coming along soon, and who wanted to meet us. Trail communication and its impact marked this day.

May 30

As Mary's blue car slowly drove away, leaving us poised at the trail entrance, a wave of homesickness enveloped me. This is the first time I would rather have been driving home than hiking. The swelling was completely gone out of my foot and it felt normal again; the sun was shining and we were well-fed and well-packed with supplies. Still, my mind and heart were speeding along in the little blue Datsun heading towards Chattanooga, Tennessee.

By early afternoon the soles of our feet were too sore to keep walking and we stopped to soak them in a stream. The two days of rest allowed our feet to become keenly tender.

Gene spotted a mother turkey crossing the trail and told me to proceed quietly and see her, too. She began making strange noises, and three babies went fluttering and staggering into the bushes. This natural scene cheered me.

May 31

I slept poorly last night as the ground caved in somewhat under my side of the tent and I ended up in a very uncomfortable groove. Feeling tired the next day, we stopped for lunch earlier than usual, finding an appealing area alongside a stream. Gene told me to nap while he prepared our dinner. We had hoped to have our meal at the new Wapiti II Shelter but now would simply stop along the way to see it.

As always, Gene hiked faster than I and breezed right past the Wapiti signpost and I had to call him back. Following a blue-blazed trail, we found a fluorescent ribbon wound around the trees, forming a closed circle around the perimeter of the area where the lean-to stood. We ducked under it, wondering aloud the reason for it. Three floor boards had been torn up in the shelter and Gene remarked, "It must have been vandals!" I noticed a pad laying on one of the three benches surrounding the circular campfire site. Thinking it was the register, I read it, finding a list of mileages recorded and gas purchased for an emergency squad vehicle. Further back was a page long statement concerning a mishap and a victim. I scanned it and then showed it to Gene, who didn't know what to make of it either. Thinking someone might come back for it, we placed it in the shelter and left.

As we began our ascent, I was jolted by the realization that something sinister had occurred at that lean-to! A terrible heaviness crept over me and I felt frightened here in the woods. I expressed these feelings to Gene but he dismissed them, saying it was pure speculation. However, the word "victim" kept coming into my mind. Soon, I started to look around as I walked, wondering if we were being followed and I even thought I heard voices. All kinds of thoughts raced through my mind. Wouldn't Mary think this was insane, after being concerned about the fear her grandparents lived in in New York City, having three locks on their side door and a baseball bat standing alongside their refrigerator for protection. Gene suggested we stay at Doc's Knob Shelter that night but I refused, practically shouting, "I will not stay at a shelter!"

After much climbing up and down, we came to a jeep road. Hearing voices, Gene, without a word, grabbed my arm and pulled me down behind tall weeds, convincing me he was only wearing the mask of calmness.

It was almost dark when we found a flat, concealed spot amongst some rhododendron bushes. Scrutinizing the area, Gene found a small water source ten feet away. The Lord provided us with a safe place and water close by.

June 1

*"Peace within us is real when we help all forms
of life to live. I love you!"*

Fog enshrouded the woods until three o'clock in the afternoon, when the sun finally broke through. Leaving Angels Rest behind, our feet hurt as we came down the near vertical descent leading to the road and Pearisburg.

Mr. Johnson, a Methodist minister, stood fueling his car and was the first person we saw to ask directions. He not only told us where the Post Office was located but volunteered to drive us there and then across town to the hostel, provided by the Holy Family Catholic Church. Entering the Post Office, I was immediately informed that two hikers had been murdered at Wapiti II Shelter, their bodies having been found yesterday by a search party. Stunned, I found it difficult to fully comprehend this devastating news and hurried out to tell Gene.

Arriving at the rectory, Father Winters warmly welcomed us and briefly alerted us to what happened. About twenty other hikers congregated together in the hostel, their young faces portraying a kaleidoscope of expressions — hurt, bewilderment, anger, fear and shock. For us, this tragedy brought back so many horrible memories of our own son's death, as he, too, was a victim of violence. We painfully identified not only with the slain hikers, but also with their parents. Our peaceful sanctuary had been shattered.

Father Winters had a private worship service at five-thirty and invited Gene and me to share it with him after I had inquired about the time for a morning prayer service. I needed quiet time, apart, for prayer and sharing the Lord's Word and the Eucharist. Praying the Lord's Prayer together, I could say, "and forgive us our trespasses as we forgive others," as I had finally been able to forgive the man who murdered our son. Now I prayed for the parents of Susan and Bob, the slain hikers.

Reporters from the television station and news media came and several hikers voiced their feelings. Listening, Sandy and I cried together. Susan Ramsey and Bob Moundford were Sandy and Neil's close friends. About ten-thirty, emotionally exhausted, I escaped into my sleeping bag, spread out in the loft of the barn. I kept waking up, though, feeling alarmed.

I tried to concentrate on the joys of that day and their meaning — the golden lady's slippers that graced the trail in one place and the special blueberry pie Rob Weisser had baked and carefully wrapped in his bandanna, leaving it as a surprise for Lisa, Pete and us. The accompanying note explained that his response to my log entry was a misunderstanding. Nevertheless, throughout the night, my mind insisted on going back to the young couple whose lives were brutally ended.

Why, God, why?

June 2

In the morning Father Winters met with all the hikers and advised couples not to return to the trail until the police apprehended a suspect. There was a possibility, however remote, that couples were more vulnerable.

He graciously offered his kitchen facilities, permitted the use of his stereo and kept the church open for everyone, hoping to help restore their inner calm and ease the congestion in the hostel.

One couple left for home by bus, while others planned on by-passing the next section of trail. Four men headed for the trail having decided that there is safety in numbers. What should we do?

Until now, our reasons for hiking the Appalachian Trail were easily explained. Our original dream was to hike the trail when we both retired. However, our son's death made us acutely aware of the swiftness of life. We became less conservative; our priorities changed. We desired to grow — to grow in awareness, courage, simplicity and sensitivity. Along the way, though, we gradually realized our journey is part of a master plan. I wondered, "What is God's reason for our hiking the Appalachian Trail at this time?"

June 3

Two days passed with no new developments or leads and Gene felt we must make a decision. Sandy and Neil spoke with us, alone and together, sharing their feelings with us. Their openness and listening helped us immeasurably.

Finally, we chose to go on. Fear would not rule us! Truthfully, though, I felt internal consternation; maybe it was a stupid idea to go on.

June 4

'I can do it, if I stay calm, think and use caution. I love you.'

Leaving town on Thursday, five different people stopped us to tell us how sorry they were about the slain hikers, how ashamed they felt such a thing happened in their area and that they'd be praying for our safety. This outpouring of feeling from the townspeople touched us.

Losing our way at the Celanese Plant on the outskirts of town, we asked a boy on a motorcycle for directions. He told us to follow the road over the mountain and turn right. Hours passed before we found an Appalachian Trail blaze.

We had walked about an hour in the woods when we saw a small brown tent with a white straw hat hanging on the tip of the front pole. Gene turned and motioned me to pass by quietly, holding his finger up to his lips. Like a bolt of lightning, it struck me. One suspicious person the authorities wanted for questions was a man reportedly wearing a white cowboy-type hat. Knowing a long distance hiker does not set up camp early in the afternoon, fear almost paralyzed me. My insides trembled and, trying to accelerate, my body moved in slow motion. Only my heart raced. The next several miles were dreadful miles with my emotions running wild, instead of my long legs.

Crossing a power line easement, a narrow strip of clearing dividing the woods, Pearisburg could be seen far below us. The route of retreat was at hand and almost irresistible. We could easily head straight down the mountain. But, looking into Gene's eyes, it was evident that this was not the way for us. He then tried to convince me that one of the hikers he briefly met in Pearisburg was wearing a large white hat and that it was most likely him.

That evening Gene carefully selected a very secluded tent site, and this became a daily precaution — tent camping, avoiding the shelters for sleeping.

June 5

Friday was an uneventful gray day and depression hovered over me.

June 6

Saturday morning the trail leveled off and became soft, with flowering mountain laurel banking either side of the path. A soft rain fell making all the leaves lustrous, as if someone had polished them. Appearing in large numbers, toads, camouflaged by their earthen colors, were seen leaping sporadically and salamanders, bright in orange skins, scurried along. Slowly our spirits began to lift; all this beauty was healing.

At four o'clock we passed Pond Mountain Shelter, about one hundred feet off the trail. Loud voices broke the silence, and we hurried past, unobserved. A sign read, "Four miles to Virginia Highway 42." We had to cross precarious rock formations, no doubt a challenge in dry weather, but dangerous in this wet weather. The blazes were painted in the most unlikely places. Progress was slow with Gene constantly helping me along. I felt like an anchor being pulled and lowered, always a weight.

We walked until eight in the evening, believing Highway 42 couldn't be far away. But it was. A deluge of rain bathed us as we hurriedly put up our tent for the night.

We crawled out stiff but dry and breakfasted on peanut butter sandwiches and a cup of water each. Although the sun shone, a feeling of sadness engulfed me.

Struggling up a mud slide, slipping and sliding the entire time, the whole idea of hiking seemed insane. It brought to mind what Syd wrote after his name in the log books — "Georgia to Insanity." Then I considered the fact that Syd had hiked the entire trail in 1978 and was back on it again this year.

Walking through a covered bridge built in 1916, we riveted our attention on a sleek black snake stretched out full length along one of the side boards.

At last in early afternoon, we emerged onto Highway 42. Imagine, it had taken us seven and one-half hours to go four miles.

Later, eating lunch outside the small grocery store in Newport, an Emergency Medical Technician came over to talk with us. He told us no one had been charged with the crimes yet, and also remarked how difficult it was to evacuate someone off Suicide Mountain when an accident occurred there. This was great to hear after our safe passage over it.

Encamped on the crest of Sinking Creek Mountain, heavy footsteps signalled someone rapidly approaching, and I peered out of the tent. A male hiker, sporting a large white hat, appeared and stopped to inquire about a source of water. My heart began to pound. "Oh, God, how I wish this fear would leave me!"

Gene recognized the young man, though, as the one he briefly met our first night in Pearisburg. The man had not stayed overnight at the hostel, as a friend picked him up shortly after Gene met him. Anxious to find water before nightfall, he didn't linger to talk with us. Again Gene tried to reassure me that the hat on his head was, indeed, the very one we had seen hanging on the tent pole in the woods.

Sleeping lightly, I felt an animal brushing against the tent as it crawled around. Night sounds awakened me several more times and then ants infiltrated our tent and made a nuisance of themselves.

June 8

Gene was up early and got things underway before I made my appearance to find a dry morning, hot coffee and a stone seat overlooking Sinking Creek Valley. What a nice beginning to a day.

The guidebook mentioned the difficulty of the rocks in this area, but after Suicide Mountain I knew we would manage. Walking, we found water and stopped to bathe, the first time in three days. Skim milk and half an apple comprised our snack.

Late morning we came upon the man with the white hat, camped alongside the trail. Dave said he had hiked until nine-thirty and then slept in his hammock. Having rested poorly, he stopped to rest some more. He went on to tell us that after leaving the Pearisburg Hostel, he had injured his ankle and upon returning to the trail had to stop early in the day due to pain. What a relief to know who was really in that tent!

Noontime found us in a relatively flat area surrounded by the beautiful blooming mountain laurel we had been hiking between. Gene chose this for our afternoon meal and suggested I relax in the sunshine. I took out my pocket New Testament and read, "And fear not them which kill the body but are not able to kill the soul, but rather fear him which is able to destroy both soul and body."

My inner calm was being restored. My husband, the sunlight, the mountain blanketed in flowers, the trees, and the knowledge of who was in that tent — all God's gifts to me — were helping me. I reread our friend Barry's note to me, tucked in with the gold chain and cross he had sent to me for Mother's Day, and that helped me, too. How much I missed our Mary and Barry!

After lunch we hiked straight up a mountain recently burned to ugliness. The pungent smell of charred wood filled our nostrils and irritated our eyes, while the grotesque shapes of the once green forest saddened us.

Once on the top, we spent the afternoon climbing rock outcroppings along the ridge crest. At one point a slanted slab of granite, approximately seventy-five feet in distance, tested my newly acquired agility. I slowly worked my way across it, carefully planting each footstep, all the while mindful of the variegated patches of green farmlands about four thousand feet below me. Gene stood watching me and later confided he had turned to take my picture to show me what I had accomplished. However, he could not snap it for the view of me on that slanted rock left a lump in his throat and all he could do was swallow.

Coming down the mountain, we once again hiked amidst magnificent mountain laurel, all shades of the most delicate pink. This night our tent was lost in the mountain laurel and a whippoorwill serenaded us to sleep.

June 9

The whippoorwill sang revelry, off key, and we awoke smiling. Gene served me coffee in my sleeping bag before we got busy with our morning routine.

We were surprised to find Niday Shelter about ten minutes farther from our hideaway and we stopped to sign the register and read the entries. We learned Rob had to go to the hospital for a tetanus injection as he got caught on barbed wire, Matt went to the hospital for treatment of severe diarrhea and everyone mentioned the barn on 311 as the place to stop.

A wooden bridge took us over a wide creek and Gene proposed a bath and shampoo, but I declined as I felt we needed to keep moving. When we crossed the third stream and Gene again offered to stop, I jumped at the chance. Forty-five minutes later, the luxury of a clean body and shiny hair engendered a sense of euphoria in me.

Re-entering the Jefferson National Forest, we decided to lunch by Trout Creek, having already travelled eight miles.

Although the guidebook indicated it was five miles, we believed the wooden sign showing eight miles, as it had taken us four hours. We were averaging two miles an hour unless the way was rugged. Again the 1974 guidebook proved to be frustrating, as there were so many reroutes and much of the information was outdated and inaccurate.

Our afternoon was spent traversing Cove Mountain, horseshoe in shape and bumpy like a dragon's back. The rocky trail, marked by sinkholes, culminated at the Dragon's Tooth, a jagged rock formation that jutted skyward, resembling a mammoth tooth. A hiker, using caution, could climb to the crown via a crack in the rocks.

The trail was not well marked here and we descended steeply, sliding on loose gravel and rocks, before realizing we had made a mistake. It was a chore getting back up, but once we were back at the base of the Dragon's Tooth, we went in the opposite direction, proceeding for approximately another mile and a half, hiking along the crest for a way, before descending steeply into a sag, known as Lost Spectacles Gap. Now eight o'clock, we knew we had better stop, as this was the first really flat area and more climbing was in store for us. Since our water was low and none was available, supper consisted of honey on bread and a few sips of water, saving the pint of water for coffee in the morning.

It was a relief to remove our boots from our battered feet. No sooner had we lain down than we heard deer snorting.

June 10

Our day began climbing the spur on Cove Mountain, which afforded views of Catawba Mountain and Valley. The descent was difficult for about a mile and we were glad we felt fresh, especially at the narrow places, in particular, Rawies Rest, a knife-like rim of rock. In an hour we reached 311, a small grocery store and telephone. It took an hour to get through to my mother, as all the telephone circuits going into New York were busy, but the effort was worth it, as I found out my father was being discharged from the hospital after a brief stay for a recurrent bladder problem. Mother explained that Dad would have periodic treatments administered in the doctor's office. I knew that this arrangement would please Dad as he strongly disliked hospitals. Mother and I talked about forty-five minutes and loved every minute.

Then Gene and I each had a pint of ice cream, pint of milk, cinnamon rolls, and a soda. We purchased groceries and talked with a southbound hiker, who staggered in. He was recovering from a five-day spell of dysentery, supposedly brought on by contaminated water. A Miller's Lite Beer Truck pulled in and the driver smilingly agreed to mail a letter for me.

Leaving after eleven, we hiked thirteen more miles along the crest of Catawba Mountain. Although the weather was hot and windy, the way was mostly soft under our feet with gradual elevation changes and only several steep ascents and descents. What a contrast from yesterday.

When the sky darkened and thunder rolled, we quickly put up our tent fly for Gene to work under. While Gene cooked, I wrote in my log book and composed a letter to Mary.

June 11

Finished letter to Mary while enjoying morning coffee, mentioning in the letter it'd be interesting to see who the Lord sent to mail it. By nine-thirty, we knew — a lumberjack, cutting trees on some privately owned land the trail crossed. He said he'd be happy to mail it from his home that evening.

The day's hike was most pleasurable as a good portion of it was along the ridge crest. For about seven miles the trail wound along narrow Tinker Ridge, exposing fruit orchards, farmlands, suburban areas and mountains to our left and glistening Carvin Cove Lake to our distant right. Passing huge rock formations, disfigured by graffiti, we stopped to rest and eat the last of our bread and cheese. Gene's foot was troubling him and he needed to take his weight off of it. Relaxing in the shade, Gene said we'd find a restaurant when we got to Interstate 81, about an hour and a half away. By the time we climbed down from the ridge, and hiked along the pavement from which we could see waves of heat rising, we wilted. A Howard Johnson's came into sight and Gene decided we should splurge and stay in a motel and eat out, spending our last fifty dollars. This came as quite a surprise to me, as it seemed extravagant, but I quickly succumbed.

After cleaning up, we went to the Pizza Hut and indulged in a large pizza with sausage and a salad. Back in our room, Gene strung up a line and I washed all our socks and our shorts, hanging them up to dry. Hand washing didn't make them look too clean but at least they'd smell better. Meanwhile, Gene soaked his sore foot.

We called our daughter, Mary, and were not only able to speak with her but also with Barry, who is planning on meeting us in Pennsylvania on his way home from Michigan.

For a change we went to sleep late, eleven-thirty.

June 12

Awoke early to another treat, complete fulfillment in loving one another. Yesterday our physical beings were restored; this morning our emotional beings had wings.

By the time we walked to Fullhardt Knob Shelter, four and a half miles, we were drenched with perspiration from the humidity and effort and stopped to cool down, finding water in the cistern behind the shelter. A young woman and her dog came bounding up the path as it if were nothing. Dawn introduced herself and her dog, Travis. Hearing we were through-hikers, she told us she was studying forestry and planned on hiking the Appalachian Trail the next year with her dog as her companion.

About nine miles later, we crossed the Blue Ridge Parkway near the ninety-seven mile marker, and found a suitable campsite not far from the parkway. We could see the tops of the cars as they drove by but doubted our tent could be seen by the car's occupants.

June 13

The day was hot and oppressively humid and we had to force ourselves to keep moving. Along the way we soaked our tired feet in Jenkins Creek, but the best was yet to come. The Lord sent us a refreshing cloudburst as we passed through a mature forest mounting Fork Mountain. For a change, I loved walking in the rain and reveled in feeling the cool water soak my hair and saturate my clothes. Lifting my face, I eagerly received this blessing and was rejuvenated.

According to our guidebook, water was obtainable at a marked spring-house. Finding it dry, Gene ceremoniously dipped water from a rain barrel outside a vacant summer house and filled our canteens.

This was one of the few times we boiled water before drinking it.

June 14

On a back road, an elderly couple stood at the tailgate of their enclosed pickup truck, eating their breakfast. Seeing us coming out of the woods, they quickly closed everything up, hopped into the cab, locked the doors and rolled up the windows. Clearly, they were afraid of us! Knowing the gentleness and kindness of my husband, I thought how deceiving appearances can be. Discussing their reaction, Gene said it probably was our walking sticks, or reading about the murders, or maybe we looked plain ravenous. After all, both of us have been so hungry these days.

The walk to Cornelius Creek Shelter was mostly up and we were ready to stop for lunch by the time we got there. A cold stream and flowering rhododendron and mountain laurel made it most attractive.

During the course of the afternoon, we crossed the Blue Ridge Parkway several more times. Near Thunder Hill Lean-to, a small doe gracefully walked into sight but by the time I got my pack off and the camera out, she vanished. Rather than putting my pack back on, we sat down to rest and eat the last of our M & Ms.

By evening my stomach hurt from being empty. Again I mentally discarded things from my pack in order to be able to carry more food. When Gene heard I intended to send home my air mattress, he advised I first try sleeping without it, cautioning, "A good night's rest prepares you for the next day."

June 15 - 102 degrees

'Water is always refreshing. I love you.'

We registered at the entrance to the James River Face Wilderness Area by filling in a questionnaire and dropping it into the wooden box provided. Even though it was early morning, the air was very warm — even the wind was warm. The sun, filtering through the blowing leaves, created moving mosaics of light on the trail. I felt strangely lightheaded and wondered if it was due to hypoglycemia or the motion of all the trees and changing designs beneath my feet.

Each mile and each hour, the day became hotter. By noon, the woods were sweltering and our T-shirts and shorts clung to our moist bodies. The shimmering water in Matts Creek appeared to be a mirage but only until I experienced the cool water on my naked body. It didn't matter to me that this area was wide open with no trees near the banks for privacy. Sitting on a flat rock, splashing to my heart's content and laughing from relief, I exemplified the advertisement, "You've come a long way, baby!"

We emerged from the woods onto the steaming highway and a scorching one hundred two degrees temperature. Knowing of Williams Country Store a mile down the road, we felt compelled to keep walking. Once inside, air conditioning, soft music, friendly people, and ice cream revived us. A potbellied stove stood in the middle of the store, a reminder of winter days in a bygone era, when the store was a gathering place. We sat on a wooden bench, eating a pint of ice cream each, all the while enjoying conversation and the coolness.

The town of Glasgow was seven miles farther and the owners arranged a ride for us when one of their regular customers dropped in. Our package had been sent to Snowden, five miles in the opposite direction, but Gene had it rerouted to Glasgow where there were the big three — a motel, supermarket and laundromat.

June 16

The temperature again went over one hundred degrees and the air conditioner in our motel room froze over while we slowly prepared to leave Glasgow. Gene sent home his belt, using a rope to hold up his pants, and the last of his warm clothing, keeping only several T-shirts. The husband of the cashier in the supermarket agreed to drive us back to the trailhead after he finished work at three o'clock. Gene offered to pay him but all he wanted was an occasional post card to let them know of our whereabouts.

Stifling hot outside, it felt good to be back in the woods in the shade of the trees and we walked very slowly. The Appalachian Trail sign specified we were entering the George Washington National Forest with the John Hollow Shelter two and two-tenths miles away and the Punchbowl Shelter thirteen and two-tenths miles away. Gene decided it'd be wise to stay near the first shelter. Our bodies demanded water in this intense heat and he didn't want to jeopardize us.

John from Tallahassee arrived exhausted and hungry just as we were preparing supper, and we gladly shared our grilled cheese and cookies with him. He no longer carried his stove, thereby cutting down his weight, and he thoroughly enjoyed being served a warm meal. With our tent set up a distance from the shelter, John said he would be spending his first night alone in a shelter since the murders. If he was afraid, he did not show it, but the fact that he mentioned the murders disclosed they were on his mind also.

June 17

Breezes made the heat tolerable, and we were at the next shelter by noontime, where we met another hiker who called himself Gypsy. Gypsy animatedly told us how a hiker saved his life earlier in the day by giving him his water. Yesterday, parched and overcome by weakness, Gypsy collapsed on the trail, believing he'd die there. Less than a mile away from the shelter, he never realized how close he was to a beautiful cold spring. We knew his Good Samaritan had to be John, as he left earlier than we and averaged twenty miles a day. Still feeling the effects of this episode, Gypsy planned on spending the day by the spring, hydrating himself.

Later in the afternoon we cooled off in Little Irish Creek. Although shallow, the water refreshed us. I kept sponging myself, while Gene soaked his sore foot. Tiny trout darted all about us, disappearing in the shadows and reappearing in the patches of sunlight.

Bone weary, twelve hours after starting out, we made camp beside Brown Mountain Creek. On the opposite side of the stream a large deer snorted loudly and leaped into the air, disappearing into the foliage.

June 18

Early in the morning an invisible maze of cobwebs forms fragile barricades across the trail and the first one down the path becomes enmeshed in sticky filaments. Pausing to brush the broken webs off my face, I was startled by a mother grouse as she noisily flew out of a thicket off to my right. Then, one by one, five young grouse took off in flight, mimicking tiny jets in precision maneuvers. This comical scene caused me to muse on how mothers prepare their offspring for life and all its possible threats.

Lunching at Wiggins Shelter, we met a lady from the Natural Bridge Branch of the Appalachian Trail Club, who had come to sweep out the shelter and check on the condition of the outhouse and the artesian well. Reading the register, I learned that Brett had to leave the trail because of back trouble and the "Cape Codder" was leaving for several weeks of R and R (rest and relaxation).

We had heard advance raves about Mr. Bear who visits this shelter in the evening, bringing all kinds of treats with him for the hikers. Although we wouldn't see him, we thought the eighteen ninth graders and their leaders, whom we passed farther along the way, would. These young people, improperly packed and floundering, were strung out over a mile. Each group wanted to know, "How far is it to the shelter?" Assurances that they were almost there brought cheers and spurts of energy.

June 19

A young buck with velvet antlers entertained us at breakfast. Playful and inquisitive, he circled our area, peering in at us through the greenery, running away if we barely moved, but always returning, venturing a little closer each time. His curiosity seemed to dictate his behavior.

Near noontime we spotted a woodchuck sitting in the middle of the trail leading to the Priest Mountain Lean-to. Hearing us, he scampered down the middle of the path, as if leading us. The spring here was exceptionally good, and the lean-to became our lunch stop.

Moving rapidly in his descent down the Priest Mountain, Gene tripped and fell forward, cutting his hands and arm as he tried to brace himself to keep from landing on his knees. He struck his hands and forearms forcibly, flipping him over onto his back and sending him sliding down the embankment. By the time I rounded the bend, Gene,

77

embarrassed and bleeding, was attempting to get back onto the trail. Refusing first aid, we continued our descent, using more caution. At Highway 56 we took a mile detour to an old-fashioned General Store-Post Office combined, where whole wheat bread, cheese, milk, Spam and ice cream were available. The clerk, a woman in her sixties figured our bill by adding the prices on a heavy piece of brown paper spread out on the counter. She invited us to sit on barrels and visit awhile, explaining she had always lived and worked in Tyro. A farmer stopped in and, after listening awhile, he offered to give us a ride back to the trail, which we gladly accepted.

We had ascended several miles, when thunder began rolling in the heavens, prompting us to immediately choose a place and get set up. It was none too soon. The storm hovered directly overhead for half an hour. Lightning illuminated our tent numerous times as thunder boomed unmercifully. What a relief to hear the storm begin to move on, leaving only raindrops. In the distance, the fury of the storm echoed throughout the mountains and I fell asleep thinking of Bob and Susan, the slain hikers.

June 20

'ROCKS, ROCKS, ROCKS! They hurt my feet, but today I choose to enjoy rock climbing. I love you.'

It was a long haul up Three Ridges. The stinging nettle grew in profusion and scratched our legs and arms as we worked our way up the switchbacks. The Priest Mountain, rising mightily out of the mist, loomed before us as we stood on Castle Rock Outlook. We felt amply rewarded.

Along the way, we met two separate groups of club members working on the trail. One crew repainted the blazes, while the other group tackled the weeds. They said "ridge-runners" were distributing apples to the hikers, but we never did meet them.

The six miles in the afternoon were over a jumble of rocks. The rocks slowed us down and were hard on our feet.

That night, reading our guidebook, I began to feel defeated. It was eleven and a half miles to Rockfish Gap, all described as rocky terrain. Sensing my discouragement, Gene raised the question of attitude and how one's attitude makes the difference between success and failure. He pointed out that I couldn't change the rocks but I could change my attitude towards them. After our long talk, I feel asleep thinking, "I choose to enjoy rock climbing." What a challenge!

June 21

The day was clear, cool, sunny and windy — a perfect hiking day. What a gift to us! The rock climbing magically turned into fun, convincing me attitude does make a difference. I chose to like rock climbing and it happened. Gene took several pictures of me scrambling up the rocks to record this change and I, in turn, took one of him on the cliffs.

The breeze was brisk in Humpback Gap along the Blue Ridge Parkway, where we ate our lunch. As it was Father's Day, I told Gene I'd walk the half mile to the Visitor's Center down the parkway for water while he rested on the grass. Without my backpack, I felt as though I could almost run.

Reaching Rockfish Gap mid-afternoon, three super highways and speeding traffic abruptly brought us face to face with the fast-paced world we temporarily left. We decided to stay at the Holiday Inn where Howard intended for us to have a special dinner as his treat. In Glasgow, we had received a letter from him containing a credit card certificate, good for up to fifty dollars, to eat at the Holiday Inn at Rockfish Gap.

The package Gene forwarded here had not arrived and that meant shampooing my hair with soap, resulting in a dull mess. Noting a band was entertaining in the dining room and everyone looked dressed up, we decided to postpone our treat until the next day and, instead, went to Howard Johnson's where, to our disappointment, the service and food were mediocre.

Returning to our room, we called my dad, Gene's mother and our daughter, who was now back at home taking care of our house and beginning a new job at Erlanger Medical Center, nursing adults rather than children.

We went to sleep listening to the hum of the air conditioner rather than the song of the birds.

June 22

Gene tentatively questioned the advisability of temporarily by-passing Pennsylvania to help us to catch up to our original time schedule. However, listening to my strong feelings about progressing in the natural order of states, he dropped the idea. Gene felt the need for a day's rest but I felt trapped in a motel, so we compromised, deciding to go into Waynesboro to pick up groceries and our package at the Post Office, and then stop for our lunch treat from Howard, returning to the trail later in the day.

As we walked into Waynesboro, six miles off the trail, a small red car stopped and offered us a ride. The young woman, Lynn, had been driving out of town when she spotted us, turned around and headed back into town, explaining she and her husband were building a home near the trail and often gave hikers rides. What a Godsend, as traffic was heavy and the concrete was hard on Gene's sore foot.

Chores completed in Waynesboro, we called Al's Cab and gladly paid three-fifty to get out of town. Back at the Holiday Inn, we learned to our dismay, the dining room was closed on Mondays.

Entering the Shenandoah National Park, we stopped to sign the register, and reading the list of names of Appalachian Trail hikers already gone by, we recognized many. Our smiles turned to frowns when we found Neil's name but not Sandy's. The next one hundred miles promised a change of pace — graded trails, abundant wildlife, campgrounds and several restaurants practically on the trail.

Late in the afternoon we scrambled over a mass of loose

rocks. The caution, "WATCH FOR SNAKES," emblazoned in big bold white letters on the stones sent our adrenalin flowing, keeping us in a state of heightened awareness.

Nighttime was spent on Calf Mountain, tenting in a rocky area amongst some stunted pine trees, overlooking the city of Waynesboro. Alone on this mountain, the myriad of lights, sprawling beyond to the south of us, flickered in mute testimony to humanity's presence. The gentle wind, the Lord's Spirit, was our only company. Once again I felt free.

Gigantic white radar discs and antennas, belonging to the Virginia State Police, all strategically positioned, were starkly silhouetted against the black, star-studded sky, making it easy to imagine we were on another planet.

June 23

'I can know myself when I can sit quiet and bring forth my inner feelings.'

This illusion was reinforced the following morning. Vacant tractor seats, each mounted on a metal post set into the grass, formed a large circle, an outdoor forum, a celestial meeting place.

That evening, pitching our tent about one hundred yards before the summit of Blackrock Mountain, Gene was busy preparing our supper, while I sat inside the tent to write in my journal to avoid being distracted by the bugs. Hearing a rustling sound, I looked up, expecting to see Gene. Instead, there stood a magnificent rust-colored doe two feet away. She walked slowly, pausing to nibble on the ferns, seemingly oblivious to us.

After this surprise, Gene came to the door of the tent and called, "Room service." Grinning, he handed in our aluminum bread pan, containing a hot grilled cheese sandwich and a cup of tea. The impromptu "silver serving tray" was also my wash basin and laundry tub. This treat brought back the memory of room service we once enjoyed at the Hyatt Regency. As deluxe as that was, this was superior;

this service was performed out of love and became a ritual on the evenings the bugs were overbearing or the weather wet.

June 24

At noontime we walked into a campground a half mile off the trail. Hot showers (five minutes for fifty cents), a laundromat and grocery store awaited us. Meeting a Boy Scout Troop from Virginia, we spoke with them awhile, during which time their leader asked to photograph us to show what through-hikers looked like.

Sitting under the shade of a tree, we were feasting on swiss cheese, bread, potato salad, milk, baloney (for Gene), plums and ice cream, when Corrie, Brian and Gypsy arrived and joined us. It gave us pleasure to share our food with them.

Later in the day the trail became rocky and Gene's foot bothered him quite a bit. He didn't complain but I could see he favored his right foot and had furrows in his brow.

We stopped at seven in the evening finding a good place in a grove of young oak trees well off the trail.

June 25

'If a smile is real, it will be there when it shouldn't be. I love you!'

Today was a sultry day remembered well because of all the weeds, bugs and insect bites. Working his way through overgrowth thigh high, Gene almost stepped on a rattlesnake lying directly on the trail in a sunny, grassy spot that had been pressed down. Startled, Gene gasped, stepping backwards. Fortunately, the reptile was preoccupied with devouring a forest creature hanging out of its jaws. In an urgent tone, Gene commanded me to stay close behind him and walk through the taller weeds bordering the trail. Relieved to safely by-pass this dangerous species, we quickened our steps. All along we had checked fallen trees before stepping over them by repeatedly banging our walking sticks on the bark and exercised alertness around rocky areas, but now we knew we had to be equally watchful in brushy overgrown places.

Gnats kept getting into our eyes and when I paused to get one out of my eye, a hornet abruptly stung me on the leg. Gene was stung, too, only he didn't respond as verbally. All the while I kept a swisher (a branch of stiff leaves, usually mountain laurel) moving like a windshield wiper in front of my face, hoping to divert the bugs.

Towards evening we wondered if there were any clear places for camping as weeds thrived everywhere. At last Gene noted an area that looked like it was once an old road, presently overgrown. He announced, "Here's our place." Taking off his pack, he got to work. Wielding his walking stick like a scythe, he knocked down the weeds. Bugs swarmed all around us as we hastily set up our tent in the altered area.

Retreating into the tent, I sighed with relief and stretched out on my mat. My thoughts turned to all the people who work together to maintain the trail and make it pleasant. Coming through one unmaintained section of trail made me acutely aware of the remarkable service these volunteers perform.

During the night an electrical storm brought a dramatic change in the weather.

June 26

Today was absolutely invigorating — cold, clear and bug-free!

Reaching Lewis Campground about ten a.m., we purchased a fleece-lined, navy blue sweat shirt for Gene, having the wording, "Go Climb a Mountain," printed in white on the front. From this point on, he was called "The Mountain Man," as the picture on the shirt resembled my mountain man with his beard, mustache, wool cap and happy smile. I had a happy smile, too, as Lewis Campground also had hot showers for twenty-five cents for several minutes.

Skirting the Big Meadows Campground, Gene suggested we stop and rent a tent site and enjoy the novelty of a bathroom, water faucet, picnic table and benches. The ranger station was a half mile into the place, and everywhere along the way we saw people having fun, reading and relaxing. After setting up on site number P-15, a grassy place under pine trees, we walked to the camp store, about a mile farther, for fresh supplies and on the way met Corrie and Brian and invited them to share our site with us, giving them directions to it. Coming out of the store, we spotted Gypsy at the same time he saw us. He came hurrying over, his felt Robin Hood's cap angled on his forehead, waving his walking stick and calling to us. Corrie and Brian broke into broad smiles when they saw who we brought back with us. Leaving his pack with us, Gypsy left to watch for Dave by the trail. By the time they both came back, we had the frankfurters cooking and we shared supper and many laughs.

June 27

Wrapped, toga style, in his red wool blanket, his heavy staff in his hand and his black hair curling beneath an improvised hood, Gypsy resembled a prophet and appeared at our site as the sun came up. He came to wave us off, and another gorgeous hiking day began with all of us laughing heartily.

During the morning we took a half-hour rest stop to appreciate the breath-taking view of the Shenandoah Valley. Together, we sat on a rock, slowly eating a juicy orange, as we absorbed the beauty of the valley, bathed in sunlight, stretched beneath us.

We reached the Skyland Restaurant, just feet off the trail, near noontime and met Frank, another long-distance hiker, waiting for the doors to open. We three ate together, thoroughly enjoying delicious food, the panoramic view from the windows and trail talk. Fresh blueberry ice cream topped off our meal.

Our eighteen-mile day ended in Thornton Gap, where we found a lovely site amongst some mountain laurel. Gene had to awaken me for supper as I had fallen asleep writing.

June 28

Sunday was Pandora's Box, filled with surprises. The restaurant we anticipated eating breakfast in was closed. The shelter, called Bird's Nest #4, had a spigot, perfect for shampooing my hair on this sunny morning. Our lunch was purchased at a camp store and consisted of a cheeseburger, french fries, a quart of milk and a pint of ice cream each, with cookies for dessert.

The trail intersected the Skyline Drive at one of the designated scenic views for motorists. Here, we sat on a stone wall to rest. A group of interested people quickly gathered around us. As Gene answered their many questions, a sleek limousine drove in and a woman, about fifty, rolled down the passenger's window to hear. Listening, she appeared captivated by the fact our journey was living a dream. Getting out, she took several pictures. When the tourists dispersed to their cars, the lady handed me an autographed Polaroid picture of us and shook our hands, saying we were an inspiration to her. This woman's response encouraged us beyond words. We speculated that she, too, had a special dream and now her hope of fulfilling it had been restored.

Our day ended on South Marshall Mountain. Perched on a rocky ledge overlooking the Shenandoah Valley, we watched the sun slowly sink behind the Massanutten Range. The sky glowed a golden peach, gradually becoming a pink-purple hue. Twilight unfolded, transforming the sky and ridge into multishades of blue. The evening star gleamed solitary in the heavens. The mooing of cows arose from the farmlands beneath us, emphasizing the stillness. Exquisitely subtle, the blues deepened into dark purple and then into black. Ever so gently, night cloaked us with a mantle of serenity What a finale to such a beautiful week.

June 29

The morning's walk took us out of the Shenandoah National Park. About lunchtime we found a new shelter, complete with a sundeck and fancy outhouse. I was so impressed by the outhouse that I convinced Gene to at least go and look at it.

The hot afternoon was spent hiking through a jungle-like area just beyond the Research and Conservation Center of the National Zoological Park, where the weeds were well over my head, consuming me, and the ticks were thick, proving to be downright distasteful. Before retiring, we carefully checked ourselves over for ticks.

June 30

Linden had a small Post Office, general store and telephone. I happily called my mother, as it was her birthday, and learned my dad wasn't feeling well. Next, I spoke with Mary, only to learn she was discouraged with her new position. After five years as a pediatric nurse, Mary was now caring for adult patients with renal problems. Being a nurse, I understood and we talked at length.

My thoughts were very much with my family as we hiked along, finally stopping in Whiskey Hollow Creek, ending a fifteen-mile day.

July 1

'Love — the best way to experience the world. I love you.'

A ten-mile stretch of road walking began at Ashby Gap, Virginia. Privately owned property lined both sides of the trail, which followed the road. No trespassing signs were frequently posted on the trees, warning "No Hunting, Fishing or Trapping," "No Trespassing," "Private Land, Keep Out," and "Private Property." The message was loud and clear and we hiked along the pavement. The most effective sign, though, was the one that commanded, "Absolutely No Nothing!"

It was near the end of this road that we were warmly welcomed at the Oscannon's estate called, "Grayrock." Here, the family generously offered the through-hikers a place to sleep in their stone summer house, a hot shower, fresh eggs and goat's milk.

July 2

Before departing we breakfasted in the barn in the company of baby chicks. This was a unique dining experience for me, having been raised on Staten Island, New York.

The bushes were heavily laden with luscious ripe blackberries, perfect for plucking. Tasting their sweetness, we ate as many as we collected. A storm was threatening but, instead of heading down the trail, we went deeper into the bushes as the biggest and best blackberries were always only an arm's reach away. Moments later, though, a downpour left us dripping wet and laughing. When we finally did walk down the trail to Key's Gap, we felt like we were sloshing along in two buckets of water — our boots.

July 3 West Virginia

A gigantic sign, "Harpers Ferry - National Historical Park" effectively proclaimed this Civil War landmark. Luckily we stopped at the Post Office first, as it was closing at noon, due to the holiday weekend. Two packages arrived for us and each of us carried one in our arms as we walked down the narrow streets to the historic Hilltop House Hotel. As always, Gene sent me in to make the arrangement, saying, "You look more presentable than I." Looking at us as objectively as possible, I was convinced and complied with his instructions. This accomplished, a porter eagerly escorted me outside saying, "I'll carry your bags for you." He disregarded my gentle warning, "But I have been carrying my own the whole way." Momentarily flustered by my unique luggage, he rallied and gallantly carried in my backpack and box.

Shortly after getting settled, this same person knocked on our door to announce we had company waiting for us in the downstairs living room. From the look of disbelief on his face and his rounded eyes, we instinctively knew who was there — Whiskey Dave and Gypsy.

July 4

What do some backpackers do when they are in a historical town inundated by a driving rain? Doing what comes naturally, we donned our rain-gear and went sightseeing, splashing in all the puddles like two children. Then we browsed in the bookstore before returning to the Hilltop to take our first daytime nap in a soft bed.

July 5 Maryland

The drizzly day made everything damp and gray looking. Crossing over the Sandy Hook Bridge, we took a picture of Harpers Ferry off in the distance. On the Maryland side of the bridge, the trail was poorly marked and strewn with garbage and broken glass. However, this was only for a short distance.

Farther along, the trail ran parallel to the C & O Canal, presently coated with a moss green glaze. A mother duck, followed by five ducklings, slowly swam along the opposite bank, giving the impression of gliding on green glass. The trail here was very flat and the trees on either side of the trail very tall. We met a man who told us to be certain we saw the paw paw trees growing in this area.

The climb up to Weverton Cliffs was by switchbacks and not bad at all. On top we met a couple, one of whom was an Appalachian Trail volunteer, who enthusiastically encouraged us. We felt satisfied knowing we at least spoke with someone from the Appalachian Trail Headquarters, as we had been very disappointed when we found it closed for the holiday weekend.

July 6

The state of Maryland provided a restroom with showers just feet off the trail. Passing this unusual provision, Gene chose to sit under the trees and daydream while I blissfully showered.

Late morning we entered the George Washington State Park and visited the first monument erected in honor of George Washington back in 1827. Shaped like an old-fashioned milk jug, it was made entirely of gray stones. The American flag flew on one side and the Maryland state flag on the other side. Walking away from this simple memorial, I almost stepped on a copperhead snake. My reaction surprised us both. Instead of screaming or running, I called Gene to see it. A while later, we spotted a scarlet tanager in its breeding plumage—its flame red body artfully transported by black wings.

Low on energy, we took a break and ate the whole pound of dietetic hard candy Gene's sister, Joanne, sent to us in Harpers Ferry. Two hours later we stopped for the evening and simultaneously became ill. Gene headed for a thicket of trees and began having diarrhea. I developed severe abdominal bloating and pain. At first I thought a cup of hot tea would help us, but doubled over in distress. Gene put up the tent by himself and I crawled in. He followed very quickly, not even bothering to tie up our food bag. Feeling miserable, we concluded the water we drank was contaminated. The question, "How will we contact my sister, Teddy, in time to tell her we are sick and would not be able to meet her as we had planned?" was left unanswered.

July 7 Pennsylvania

Today was my forty-seventh birthday and we both awoke feeling one hundred percent better and agreed the candy must have been the culprit; our misery was self-inflicted by overindulgence.

Coming to a scenic view overlooking the Cumberland Valley, the story *Christy* flashed into my mind. Now, hang gliders used this site as a point of departure but, presently, none were in the air.

At Pen Mar County Park, considered the halfway point on the Appalachian Trail, Gene prepared a big pot of rice pudding for our main meal. Afterwards, stretched out on a park bench, I observed with fascination the myriad leaves overhead as they submitted to the stiff breezes and I smiled, enjoying the sunshine and my birthday. What a meaningful way to celebrate life—learning life hiking the Appalachian Trail.

About four o'clock we crossed the Pennsylvania state line, entering the seventh state in our journey. In Michaux Forest Gene located the spring the young hiker told him about. The water turned out to be the best in all of Pennsylvania. After this, water became scarce.

July 8

Early morning, with its dewy freshness and sense of new beginning, is my favorite time of day and this morning, in particular, held special promise as my sister would be joining us today. In our eagerness, we hiked the ten and a half miles to Caledonia State Park in seven hours. The first structure we saw was the summer playhouse where a matinee was in progress. Peering through the screened-in spaces, we could see the performers on stage. Across the highway, we located the visitor center where we had arranged to meet Teddy, expecting it to be a comfortable air-conditioned building. Instead, there stood a small log cabin with a "Closed" sign hanging on the door. Seeking a park ranger, he advised us the Trailways Bus stopped in front of the Thaddeus Stevens Museum. I sat on a nearby bench to wait while Gene walked down the highway to a small store. At a nearby table, a family set up a fabulous picnic spread, complete with china.

At last I could see a bus barrelling down the road and I jumped up, excitement flooding my being. But the bus never slowed down and my heart sank. Returning to my seat, anxiety crept in and I decided to talk to God. Ten minutes later another bus came, only this one approached from the opposite direction, slowed down and stopped. To my great happiness, a smiling Teddy hopped off. While we hugged and greeted each other, the driver unloaded Teddy's backpack. We were now a three-member team and our adventure took on an added dimension.

Gene decided we should camp on a designated site in the state park and take advantage of the modern conveniences, a gentle way to initiate Teddy to trail life, as she came straight from Greenwich Village in New York City. Among other things, Teddy surprised me with a birthday treat, a fresh loaf of pumpernickel bread with a candle on it.

This night our two-man tent, with a little squeezing, became a three-person tent.

July 9

Today was an ideal first day for Teddy as there was only one long ascent, early in the day, before it became hot. From then on it was soft travels on a relatively flat area. In Gene's words, "We could dance, it was so easy." Stopping at a stream to rest, we met a group of young boys with two adult leaders. The youngsters intently watched how Gene obtained water from the shallow stream without stirring up the silt on the bottom and began quizzing him. As he responded to their many questions, demonstrating how to scoop out a deep basin and let the mud settle before drawing the water, and showed genuine interest in them, they became animated and followed him around until we left.

Towards the end of the day, the trail soil turned sandy and we noted giant-sized ant hills alongside the path. Some of them were several feet in diameter and almost as high. Imagine the maze of tunnels and the activity within these sandy hills!

Ending the day at Michner Cabin, presently locked, we found a flat area for our tent, a picnic table and a fast moving stream.

July 10

The day went better after we took time to rearrange the contents of Teddy's pack, making it easier for her to carry. I also helped Teddy put on her pack and take it off, knowing how much it meant to me when my husband assisted me. We also knew we had to slow our pace to give Teddy a chance to break in gradually, as we needed to do months earlier.

The high point of this thirteen-mile day, which ended setting up our tent in a hunters' camping area just prior to Limekiln Road, was the refreshing ice cream stop at Pine Grove Furnace Store, where we each easily ate a pint of ice cream.

July 11

This discouraging day ended remarkably. Most of the day the route was confusing, as some of the white blazes had been browned out, and we lost our way for awhile. While cooking our dinner, our gas stove blew a gasket and a ball of flames engulfed the stove. Visions of a forest fire erupted before me, but surprisingly the fire burned itself out and the macaroni was sufficiently cooked to eat.

The long climb in the afternoon proved strenuous for Teddy and she was nearly overcome by heat exhaustion. Her feet hurt her, too, adding to her misery and to our concern.

It was after seven o'clock when we hiked into Churchtown, Pennsylvania. The three miles of road walking beside fields of tall corn wreaked havoc on Teddy's feet and she hobbled along behind me, oblivious to the golden evening tide.

Our destination was Joan Ziegler's house. Joan is the postmistress for the Allentown Post Office, one of our mail drops. Not getting a response to ringing the doorbell, I went around to the back of the house and found Joan resting and visiting with her family and a guest. Minutes after introducing ourselves, we were being driven into Allentown to pick up our mail and to meet Barry. But Barry, who was to meet us in front of the Post Office, was nowhere to be seen and we felt a keen disappointment. Joan advised Gene to check at the restaurant across the street, but no one fitting Barry's description had ever been there.

Returning to her house after an ice cream stop, Joan generously invited us to set up our tent on her soft lawn and to use her bathroom. Teddy, grateful to be able to soak her battered feet, recovered her usual sunny disposition. Refreshed after my turn in the shower, I went outside to find everyone gathered around the picnic table, talking animatedly. In the darkness, I had to look closely to try to find a place to sit. Peering around at the shadowy figures, I spotted an extra person wedged in amongst the rest, and cried with excitement, "Barry!" Throwing my arms around him, talking and laughing at the same time, I hugged him repeatedly—what a wonderful conclusion.

Hours later, we crawled into our sleeping bags and Barry eased himself into Joan's hammock, set up next to our tent. How blessed we were to be received by these people!

July 12

Breakfasting at a Dutch Pantry, Barry and Gene each had a double order for breakfast. Between courses, we scrutinized all the photographs taken thus far on our trip, commenting on each picture and making mental notes of things to remember in our future pictures.

With our packs repacked much heavier, we again bid farewell to Barry and to Joan and her family. Just like the first day on the trail, Barry sadly watched us depart, only this time the trail took us down Main Street, with buildings on either side, instead of down a narrow dirt path, bordered by bare trees.

We began to cross the Cumberland Valley, flat, hot and hard on our feet with all its road walking and lack of shade trees. The "Ice Cream Lady," a legend on the trail, lived somewhere along this stretch and we watched for her house. A small neat sign, "Shipe's Watering Hole," caught our attention. Ringing the bell, a friendly, young vivacious woman responded, "You must be Madelaine." How did she know? Resting in comfortable chairs on the front porch, a cold drink in one hand and an ice cream cone in the other, we learned how Bonnie Shipe knows who to expect, (the hikers who stop naturally fill her in on who is not far behind), signed her register and shared funny stories. One account made the Ice Cream Lady ninety years old! Bob Barker, a senior hiker, happily discovered this rumor and delighted in telling us of his shocked surprise when he first met Bonnie — young, fresh and alert.

Learning of our cooking problem, Steve, Bonnie's husband, gave Gene a makeshift gasket to try on our stove. An hour was gone in no time and we had to leave these gracious people as we hoped to reach the next wooded area before nightfall.

July 13

Our day was spent climbing, crossing and descending Cove Mountain. At one of our rest stops, Teddy removed her boots to massage her battered feet and discovered three of her toe nails had turned dark. Her boots evidently lacked the necessary allowance needed for hiking downhill with a pack on. This could pose a real problem and I felt apprehensive for her and us.

At Hawk Rock we photographed Teddy overlooking the Susquehanna River, Shermans Creek and Duncannon. Beyond this point our bag of M & Ms split and we painstakingly and laughingly retrieved every last colorful candy from the rocky footway.

Later, as we walked down High Street taking us through the center of Duncannon, we stopped at the antiquated hotel to check on accommodations. Teddy and I took a brief look at the rooms, and exchanging a look of repugnance, continued on our way. The Riverfront Campground proved to be exactly right. A quiet, clean place, it had showers and plenty of space.

July 14

The major portion of the day was spent doing laundry, shopping, going to the Post Office, barber shop and resting. By four o'clock we had literally pulled up stakes and were ready to move on. The traffic was heavy as we crossed the Clarks Ferry Bridge and we had difficulty crossing US 22-322. How good it was to get back into the mountains! Up on the crest of Peters Mountain, we followed the base of its rocky spine, selecting a tent site on the pinnacle of a rock formation. We felt we were in a penthouse—windy, cool and bug-free.

July 15

I recorded very little on this day and write from our combined memories. We stopped for lunch at the Earl Shaffer Shelter (named for the first man to hike the entire Appalachian Trail) and Gene had to go three hundred fifty feet down a blue-blazed trail on the north side of the mountain to obtain water. Meanwhile, Teddy and I hunted an abundance of dead wood, knowing if we collected sufficient fuel our fire would burn long enough to cook and also to boil water for coffee.

A group of boys from a nearby YMCA camp arrived and asked Gene where he obtained the water. Directed, they scurried downhill, returning about thirty minutes later with scary details of confronting a rattlesnake. Their tale terrorized another boy who had stayed behind, and who later left the group, departing down another blue-blazed trail farther along the way. He evidently knew a shortcut back to Camp Shikellimy.

That evening we passed two of the three boys from Pennsylvania, Tim and Mickey. Rick had since left the trail. They told us about becoming full-fledged members of the Gallon Ice Cream Club back at Pine Grove Furnace and how sick it made them. Initiation into the club required a hiker to consume a gallon of ice cream in one sitting and they blamed the proprietor for the outcome. Eating that pound of candy in Virginia had taught us a hard but valuable lesson, and we weren't even tempted to join.

July 16

The Lord surprised us again, working through His people. After a long fifteen-and-a-half-mile day of hiking, which took us through St. Anthony's Wilderness, we entered Ron's Grocery Store in the village of Greenpoint and selected a supper of cottage cheese, garden tomatoes, green peppers and ice cream. The night before I had dreamt of food for the first time and, in my dream, had all kinds of salads and fruits.

As we stood in front of the store debating where to find a campsite, Russell Miller, Ranger at the nearby Boy Scout camp, stopped to talk with us. He invited us to spend the night at the Bashore Scout Reservation, Lancaster-Lebanon Council, telling us the season had ended the previous week and all the campers had gone home. Happy to accept his hospitality, we climbed into the back of his pickup truck for a new experience of riding in an open truck. Driving into the camp, Russell told us we could either set up our tent in the woods on the left or sleep in his roomy twelve foot by twelve foot tent, already set up. It wasn't hard to decide. His wife, Thelma, even offered us the use of their camper but we chose the tent for its spaciousness. However, we decided to use the camper to cook in.

After a hot shower and shampoo, the couple gave us a tour of their facilities, all the while exhibiting pleasure in their work. While sipping on freshly brewed coffee, we shared stories of our trip. Before saying goodnight, Thelma gave us sausage and butter towards our breakfast, postal cards from the camp store to send home, and sweet Lebanon baloney for our packs. This couple enjoyed giving. Thelma simply said, "That's what we're here for." Bashore Scout Reservation, promoted as "a place for all reasons...in all seasons" proved to be just that.

July 17

During the night the frogs croaked in unison and the large tent windows let in lots of fresh, damp air, and we rested comfortably. Arising early, we began "playing house" in Thelma's little trailer as Teddy and I cooked the sausage, scrambled eggs, boiled eggs to carry and boiled water for our instant oatmeal. Since our stove malfunctioned, we had been eating our oatmeal cold. There were no lumps in this oatmeal!

Thelma drove us back to the place she and her husband met us, only now we rode in the cab of the truck. Giving Thelma a bear hug, we parted with indelible memories and began several miles of road walking before the trail took us along the crest of game lands. Again I was surprised at finding myself liking Pennsylvania so much. We set up camp shortly after passing Pilgir Ruh Spring (Pilgrims Rest), where there has been a flowing spring since colonial times.

July 18

Lunch was enjoyed at a crossroads in the woods, before proceeding to walk six miles on a wide level game lands road, which was very hot since we did not benefit from the shade of the trees. Our fifteen-mile day ended with a rocky climb and Gene having to work to make us a site free of rocks.

July 19

Teddy and I soaked our feet in the cooling waters of the Schuylkill River while Gene went into Hamburg for supplies. He returned in an hour with several bags of fresh food, being able to get a ride back with a family he met in the food market. The driver did not want to accept the five dollars Gene pressed into his hand but Gene requested he buy ice cream for the children.

The intense heat made the sharp, rocky climb out of Port Clinton difficult for Teddy and I felt concerned for her. By the time we reached Winsor Furnace, she looked devastated. The bugs were heavy and seemed to focus mostly on her as she sat at our campsite frantically waving her arms to ward them off. Visibly irritated, she bemoaned the fact I hadn't warned her about bugs ahead of time. I asked Gene to help me quickly set up the tent so we could get Teddy out of her misery.

During the night, Teddy awakened Gene to tell him a big cat was getting into our food bag. Half asleep, Gene stumbled out into the night to properly tie up our food bag. Being hot and tired, this night he had taken a chance and simply hung the food off a broken branch, instead of between two trees. A full grown raccoon was about to capitalize on his mistake.

July 20

'Think positive. Even among the rocks a place was provided for us to rest! I love you.'

98

Today was the turning point for Teddy. We were hiking along the ridge near Hawk Mountain when the rains came. The bugs disappeared, the air turned cool and, to my intense pleasure, Teddy was singing and dancing down the trail. How happy it made me to see my sister, once again, smiling at six p.m. in the evening.

For the next several hours we were caught in a heavy rainstorm. The extremely rocky terrain became slick and twilight made it difficult to see the rocks well. My Mountain Man miraculously found a small clearing amongst the rocks, a space barely large enough for our five by seven tent. My sister and I agreed contentment is being snug in a dry sleeping bag, munching on a granola bar for supper.

July 21

In daylight we spotted the "No Trespassing" sign, posted by a church group. We all grinned, as we knew the Lord provided this place for us.

Tomorrow was Teddy's birthday and we were amazed to find ourselves celebrating at Gambrinus Restaurant, indulging in a full course meal at eleven-thirty in the morning. This quaint Bavarian-type restaurant caught our immediate attention once the trail left the woods to cross the highway. Feasting like we did, though, we found it difficult to resume a good pace.

Carefully working our way over the "knife-edge" on Blue Mountain, we witnessed a rapidly approaching thunderstorm. A streak of lightning shattered the sky and my poise, as there was no immediate place to escape to. To proceed ahead, as quickly as possible, was our leader's decision. Soon a mass of dark gray clouds dramatically passed low over our heads, tumbling noiselessly down into the valley beneath us, blocking the countryside and houses from view. Large rain drops fell upon us as we proceeded to safety.

Teddy's party and the sudden storm made this a memorable day for the three of us.

July 22

'The only way to get up this mountain is with help. I love you.'

Arriving in Lehigh Valley shortly before noon, a man in the auto repair shop allowed us to put our backpacks in his office and string up a line behind his building to dry out our socks before we walked a mile down the road to a restaurant and food market.

The afternoon's climb was a notable accomplishment as it took us over Death Mountain, devoid of any grass or trees. From a distance, this low mountain appeared to be a brown, barren pile of rock and dirt, some 1,200 feet high. Halfway up the trail, we encountered a hiker descending. Stopping to greet us and to wipe his brow, he said his legs were still trembling. His comment puzzled us as we still didn't realize the challenge awaiting us—rock climbing, with small handholds and only narrow places for our feet. Slowly we advanced, carefully following our leader, as no longer was there a definite way. Up and up we went. Positioned on a ledge, I turned around to see how Teddy was faring and encouraged her to get where I was, and once there, helped her out of her pack.

Below us was a breathtaking panoramic scene. Miniature cars and trucks moved on a ribbon of highway. The Lehigh River gleamed in the sunlight, winding between rolling hills and distant mountains. The extreme height did not frighten me. Four months ago, I would have been petrified. Instead, my sister was petrified. "This is not what I expected the trail to be like," Teddy uttered. "I think I made a terrible mistake." Quietly I reassured my sister, "We are going to make it." Removing my pack, I tied the rope Gene tossed down from his position about ten feet higher to my pack frame and helped guide it as he hoisted it up. We did the same with Teddy's pack. With packs and walking sticks up, it was Teddy's turn. Gene directed her every step, repeatedly admonishing her to stay calm and to concentrate on her movements. There was a lump in my throat as I watched her bravely and cautiously proceed and sighed with relief when

Gene grasped her hand. With my turn completed, we all rested, and even took pictures, before the final ascent. Having taken his pack up first, Gene came back to assist Teddy. He warned us to brace ourselves for the stiff wind on top. After guiding Teddy safely over, Gene returned and eased into my pack and I into Teddy's all the while teasing me how light my thirty-six pound pack was compared to his fifty pounds plus pack. Together, me behind, we scaled the uppermost boulders.

That night, Gene laughingly confessed his worst fear of the day, "How will I ever manage two hysterical women?"

July 23

Hiking along a narrow tree-lined grassy path, my right boot suddenly caught on a concealed jagged stone, propelling me forward. The right side of my face forcibly struck a large flat rock with a resounding crack. Blood spurted out and I lay there under the weight of my pack thinking, "My jaw is broken. This is the end of my journey!" Struggling to raise up, I called to Teddy who was not far ahead. She responded immediately and yelled, "HAZEN!" at the top of her lungs. The loudness of her voice and choice of his first name startled me. Teddy pulled off my pack and quickly applied water and pressure to my face.

As they attended to me, Dave and Englishman Bill came along. After hellos, Dave said, "You're sitting in the middle of the trail scowling and bleeding, some way to meet someone I have been following for miles." They talked with us, telling us about meeting Cindy Ross and having the opportunity to preview her manuscript about her Appalachian Trail journey, all the while helping us to act like nothing much happened. It was the best medicine.

Scrutinizing my bruised and swollen face in a tiny mirror, I thanked God this accident didn't happen yesterday. Having collected ourselves, we began walking. From here on there was nothing but rocks, rocks and more rocks—every conceivable size and shape strewn along the trail. Our feet became weary and tired; our spirits drooped. Near the end of the day Teddy commented, "Surely there is an easier way to enjoy nature." Perhaps, but this day, the trail taught me a remarkable lesson. I can literally fall flat on my face, get up and go on.

July 24

'A good leader is efficient only when he is tuned in to the feelings of the team. I love you.'

I awoke feeling battered and out of sorts. Teddy awoke to unhappily announce she would be leaving the trail at the Delaware Water Gap as her feet pained her all night long. Gene awoke weary and didn't say much. Once again rocks were eroding our morale, only this time they were small rocks. Plodding along, our feet turned every which way, bending and rolling with the contour of the rocks.

By one o'clock we were hot and out of water, and Gene left Teddy and me to find fire wood, while he went down a blue-blazed trail in search of water. Believing the Lord would provide, we set everything out, ready to prepare our dinner. A smiling Gene returned with lots of cold water and a new snake story. With that, we heard bellowing that kept getting louder and louder, until we realized a hiker was yelling obscenities at the rocks. Sighting us, he looked embarrassed and apologized for his exasperation. We had first met Dave at Pearisburg and then again at Lehigh Valley. He said he was leaving the trail at the Delaware Water Gap, where his father would pick him up and offered to drive me to a dentist, after hearing of my fall. However, I declined his kind offer.

By late afternoon the nature of the trail drastically changed. The rocks ended and we walked on soft earth.

Twelve hours after starting out, Teddy and I spotted our leader standing at the edge of the dirt country road, smiling widely and pointing horizontally with his walking stick, his red bandanna flapping on the one end. He had chosen a site for the night; it was time to rest.

July 25

Sitting around our morning campfire, leisurely talking and eating our macaroni and cheese breakfast, Teddy expressed second thoughts about leaving the trail. I told her Gene and I never made a decision when we were overtired and impatient. Morning time was for us the best time for deciding matters.

The trail off the ridge, giving us our first glimpse of the Delaware River, took us through pines and rhododendron and alongside a pond, adorned with open water lilies. The beauty of the morning, the cushioned trail and the fact we made it across Pennsylvania together affected us positively. All three of us were smiling and in the best of spirits.

The Mountain House stood at the top of the hill, appearing spotless and inviting. Old-fashioned rockers, arranged on a wide veranda, waited for weary travellers, and I eagerly went in to make room arrangements, a double room for Gene and me and a single room for Teddy, each having double exposures with screens. Antique furniture, fresh cut flowers and everything clean and polished appealed to me and made me feel good.

After showering and opening our package from home and an extra one from Mary and Barry with a brand new stove in it, Teddy and I gathered all our soiled clothing and headed to East Stroudsburg via a bus. Gene felt it was more important to sit on the porch and rest, and in retrospect, he was right. Teddy and I went to the laundromat first, then Wau Wau's for lunch, the grocery store next and, while I waited outside, Teddy went into K-Mart. We finished up by attending a worship service at St. Matthew's Church but left before Communion as we didn't want to miss the last bus out of town. However, we ended up waiting an hour at the bus stop and began to think we had, indeed, missed it.

Dinner, consisting of fresh melon with lemon, orange bread with butter, veal with egg noodles and a vegetable dish, hot peach pie and coffee, was scrumptious but sparse for our Mountain Man and he left the table hungry.

The day ended with everyone gathered in the living room to listen to another guest play his guitar. All the while, Teddy and I mended our worn shorts.

July 26 New Jersey

Before we left the Mountain House, Cathy and Maryann, known as the California Girls, came up to our room to visit as they were staying at the hostel nearby. Then Whiskey Dave surprised us, giving me a bear hug, and we sat on the front porch for a brief spell. He had read about my fall in one of the log books and was concerned. Although we only saw other through-hikers on occasion, there was a strong common bond linking us all together.

At noontime we crossed the Delaware River and entered New Jersey, a very exciting moment for us as New Jersey had been our home state for over twelve years. Sitting on the lawn outside the Visitors' Center, we celebrated with fruit and homemade cookies, sent to us by Mary. Spotting two southbound hikers, we smiled and motioned for them to join us. Mary and Tom, a nurse and a doctor, began their hike at Katahdin and swapping stories with them made for lively conversation.

The climb up to Sunfish Pond along Dunnfield Creek was remarkably easier than it had been twenty years earlier, when Gene and I undertook our very first overnight backpack trip together, hiking this section of trail.

Now a conditioned member of our team, Teddy toted a full thirty-pound pack. When she decided to continue on with us, she expressed the desire to carry her full share of the burden. That evening Gene taught a smiling Teddy how to erect the tent in the rain. Once inside the tent, Gene served each of us a cup of steaming soup and a hot grilled cheese sandwich. Our eating utensils and pots (blackened by the wood fires) now had a strange soft luster, as back at the Mountain House Teddy had scoured everything until it glowed.

July 27

'In the woods I can relax and collect my thoughts and enjoy myself. I love you.'

Teddy and I thoroughly enjoyed our hot morning coffee and the fact that we didn't have to first find wood to build a fire. The new stove, which we called the "Gift of the Magi," because we knew it was sent out of love and meant a sacrifice on Mary and Barry's part, caused Gene some grief. The burner would not shut off completely until Gene extinguished it with his breath. A few days later, though, this frustrating problem corrected itself when, out of aggravation, Gene turned the stove upside down and a fine spray of fuel spewed from the nozzle until the stove cooled sufficiently to reduce the pressure within.

The New Jersey woods with low trees, plentiful green grass and open spaces, affording many views of the countryside, pleased us immensely. I experienced a sense of freshness and gentleness.

During the morning we spent a delicious time picking and eating blueberries. After this fruit stop, a granola snack at the firetower and an early spaghetti dinner on the Kittatinny Ridge, Gene commented, "At last, I am full after the lean weekend." Laughter erupted, as the irony of having to return to the woods to be satisfied struck us funny.

July 28

Hiking into Culvers Gap, we talked about and envisioned the homemade bread and pastries we would indulge in when we reached Worthington Bakery located on Route 206. These sweet imaginings and the yeasty aroma of freshly baked bread quickened our steps. What a letdown to find all the stores on Route 206 closed! Seeing a bread truck stop in front of a tavern down the road, we hurried there only to find it also closed. Determined, Teddy and I went around back to the kitchen entrance and asked the lady if she'd be willing to sell us some bread. She graciously sold us two loaves of fresh rye bread.

Our hike through Stokes State Forest and up Sunrise Mountain was a gentle walk, with an elevation change of only seven hundred feet in five miles. Near Mashipacong Shelter, surrounded by litter, we obtained ice cold water from a pump which was located near a paved road. The road explained the litter.

At seven p.m. our sixteen-mile day ended abruptly at the base of a very rocky ascent. The last four miles had been rough and Teddy's feet gave out. Observing her strained, forlorn appearance, I knew she had reached her limits, although she did not complain. Besides, dusk was settling in quickly and it was beginning to rain.

There wasn't a good tent site in this swampish area and our Mountain Man had to eke out a spot for us here, right beside the trail, but only after he first explored the area beyond the ascent, preferring to be on higher ground, if possible. The rain and tiredness convinced us to skip supper. We were simply grateful for a dry, relatively soft place to lie down and I fell asleep immediately. Gene lay there, wide-awake, thinking about the predicament we would be in if it rained heavily. Our leader, as always, shrewdly anticipated situations and possible solutions.

July 29

Recognizing Sawmill Lake from the crest, we felt excited hiking down into High Point State Park. Tomorrow was our son's birthday and nineteen years ago we had celebrated his fourth birthday, here at campsite #23 during our first family camping experience. At that time, our daughter had invited as many children as she could round up to come to Steven's party. How meaningful it was to us to reach High Point at this time.

As we walked towards the camping area, Ken Karnas, director of the Youth Conservation Corps, stopped to talk with us and asked us if we would be willing to share our

Appalachian Trail experiences with a group of teenagers. The youths were very interested and receptive and asked many questions after our impromptu talk.

Next, Ken surprised us by saying he wished to do us a favor. Within minutes, we were driven to and from a Shoprite Supermarket three miles down the road. Upon our return to the park, we had a festive lunch of turkey and ham sandwiches, whole milk and a coconut birthday cake, all the while reminiscing about the years we raised our children.

In the afternoon we walked through the woods where Gene had taken Steven and his friend, Rickey, on their first backpack trip fifteen years ago. Gene even pointed out the place they had slept under the stars.

Seven miles of road walking took us through rolling farmlands and flat areas growing sod, while strong breezes cooled us and unusual cloud formations entertained us. A great sense of peacefulness flooded my being and I felt very close to my husband, who was a half mile down the road ahead of me, and to our son, who no longer walked on our earth.

This was, indeed, an unusual day on the trail.

July 30 New York

The coolness of the clear morning and the fact we were crossing pasturelands made the five miles of country road walking to Wawayanda State Park most pleasant. Passing along the edge of a barnyard, a baby calf could be seen nuzzling its mother, its clean, soft coat glistening in the sunlight. Could this animal be but a few hours old? Gene felt it was.

A steep thousand-foot climb took us back into the woods, where we found a lunch stop under some huge hemlocks. Stiff breezes cooled us as we ate.

Reaching Warwick Turnpike about five-thirty, Teddy and I walked one-fourth mile up the road to a brick home in quest of water. There a man allowed us to fill our canteens using his garden hose. Retracing our steps, we were about to enter the woods again when we spotted a sign advertising a wayside fruitstand five hundred feet to the right. What a grand surprise! We ate several pieces of fruit and selected choice plums, nectarines, tomatoes and green peppers to carry with us. The added weight was a welcomed burden.

Hearing we would reach the outlet of upper Greenwood Lake in two and one-half miles, where we could camp and where there'd be lots of water for Teddy to soak her feet and for me to shampoo my hair, we two suddenly generated speed, but an hour later, stagnant looking water ended our plans.

In a densely wooded area we spotted an antiquated car with its windows broken out, permanently parked in a gully, encircled by tall trees and undergrowth. This strange sight caused us to puzzle over how it ended up where it was.

Miles later, still no water source was to be found—the drought continued. In near darkness, Gene and I set up the tent while Teddy fixed tomato and cheese sandwiches.

July 31

"A few moments of quiet in time of stress is helpful."

A fiery sunrise affirmed the beginning of a sunny hot day. All morning we scrambled over the irregular rocky crest, high above Greenwood Lake, and our water supply was nearly depleted by the time we found Roger's Oasis. A small table, two chairs, a gallon jug of orangeade and the *New York Times* seemed like an illusion in the woods, until we sat on the chairs and satisfied our thirst. A stranger's unusual kindness and ingenuity gave us a much needed respite.

Several hours later, Teddy and I sat in the middle of the trail, fanning ourselves, while Gene went down a side trail hunting water but again the stream was barren. Returning with an empty water carrier, his unsmiling face was wet with perspiration. Grimy and sweaty, we quietly continued along the ridge, the sun beating down hard upon us.

Once off the ridge, though, we had a delightful surprise awaiting us, Valley View Restaurant on Mt. Peters. This was the place Mary and Tom (the couple we met at the Delaware Water Gap) told us not to miss. A two-hour break in an air-conditioned restaurant worked wonders for us, and before leaving the waitress even filled our canteens with ice water.

Evening time we entered Sterling Forest where the trail was paved with broken beer bottles and litter. The deplorable condition of the trail depressed me, and the area where we stopped to camp didn't help matters any. Everything was brown and brittle; the ground felt like a dry sponge.

Gene announced a round table discussion before retiring. Our leader wanted suggestions on how we could hike more efficiently. He calculated in order to reach our goal in Maine, we'd have to begin doing fifteen-mile days. Teddy and I agreed to try to hike nine miles by noontime. We'd press hard! The pressure was on, but we were doing it to ourselves.

August 1

Arising at five, we were out of our sleeping bags before the first bird peeped. I did not sleep well. In my dreams I was trying to hurry but could not. It startled me to think maybe I couldn't reach Katahdin. Each time I awoke I thought of what changes needed to be made to save time. Limiting our rest stops to two brief ones, cut our lunch period to an hour, eat a cold breakfast and forgetting about middle-of-the-day shampoos would help.

We ate our oatmeal cold, along with a slice of bread and cheese and were walking by six-thirty. The early hours were quiet and cool, and we moved at a rapid pace for the first two hours, rested briefly and then continued up to the ridge. Low on water, we rationed ourselves as Gene told me to go easy on the water, as he felt Teddy needed it most. Her body was not as accustomed to the rigors of the trail as were ours. Several times she appeared about to wilt but each time water restored her. Upon the ridge, Teddy tripped over a broken tree, wedging her leg between the stump and the tree trunk, thus preventing her from going all the way over and landing on her head. Frightened, I tugged on her pack until she was upright. First aid applied, we all laughed, as only then did we see the humor in our situation. One cannot safely rush on the trail.

Noontime, five and a half hours and six miles after starting out, we safely descended Agony Grind. The name is explicit; it was a grind.

Crossing the New York State Throughway via an overhead bridge, I could sense the presence of many people, even though only a few were visible. Entering Harriman State Park, we knocked on the door of the first house to request water. When no one responded, we helped ourselves to water from the garden hose in the backyard while two watch dogs and a cat scrutinized us. At first the dogs barked furiously but ceased when we ignored them.

A narrow cleft between rocks, Lemon Squeezer, slowed us down as Gene had to take our packs through for us. We couldn't fit with them on and it wasn't until we were through that we realized we could have walked around it, had we taken the time to investigate. Walking along, I felt discouraged thinking if I couldn't make fifteen miles a day, maybe I should leave the trail and let Gene finish by himself. At this point I felt I was a hindrance, not a good feeling.

The woods in the park were very open, the trees gigantic in height and, after all the rocky crests, the ground felt soft.

We stopped atop a plateau around six-thirty and Teddy and I erected the tent while Gene hunted unsuccessfully for water. He built a fire (as we were out of fuel) and made hot soup and boiled eggs to go with the last of our bread. The food bags were lean.

August 2

The morning was spent hiking through Palisades State Park — clean, rocky and with only few people compared to yesterday. Entering Bear Mountain State Park, a wave of nostalgia swept over me as this is where Gene and I shared some marvelous, humorous times in our courtship days. Climbing a steep ascent, we met a city couple out for the weekend to celebrate their anniversary. Stopping to talk, Teddy looked relieved to rest. The climb and the heat were taking a toll on her. By lunchtime, Teddy appeared haggard and didn't say much. Little did I know, Teddy was having similar feelings to the ones I had yesterday. She did not share these feelings until late in the afternoon after she had struggled up Bear Mountain, lagging way behind me. Tearfully, she announced she must leave the trail several weeks earlier than planned, choosing to place the team's ultimate goal above hers. Teddy's strong spirit was willing, but her body was resisting. As her sister, I knew I was going to miss her presence; as a nurse, I knew her decision was a prudent one; but, as a through-hiker I felt selfishly relieved — with one less person to be concerned about, maybe I would do better. From the first day on the trail, I learned my pace determined the miles we hiked each day.

While we sat talking, our leader waited far ahead. We reached the grounds of Bear Mountain Inn about five o'clock. People were everywhere, engrossed in their own activity. Feeling like I was in a foreign land, we walked through this throng of people. The unusual thing about it all was that people did not stare at us or even appear to notice us. In the cafeteria, we discussed Teddy's departure from Graymoor, a day away. The crowded atmosphere made our conversation even more strained. We belatedly acknowledged it wasn't fair to us or to Teddy to expect her to keep up with us, we being seasoned hikers, she a tenderfoot. Gene and I should have known better than to invite another person to join us, midway in our hike. We all agreed Teddy did great and could be proud of her accomplishment. In retrospect, we feel Maryland, Pennsylvania, New Jersey and New York are the states to increase daily mileages to make up for the difficult days in the southern states or bank miles towards the strenuous days ahead in the New England states. The trail had taught us another tough lesson.

The trail passes through the Bear Mountain Zoo, but since the gates had already been closed for the night, we walked through an underground tunnel to reach the Bear Mountain Bridge. The toll booth attendant smilingly waved us across free. The Hudson River, flowing beneath us, moved toward New York City, forty miles downstream. An exhilarating feeling swept over me.

Darkness enveloped us as we set up our tent. The night sounds differed here; distant cars, trucks, an occasional train and boat whistle could be heard. We felt fortunate to have found this camping place where, through the trees, we could see the Hudson River below us.

August 3

Breakfast consisted of a bowl of cereal without milk, but this was adequate since it was an easy four-mile walk to Graymoor. Coming across a grassy field, we could see a huge crucifix off in the distance and knew we had reached our destination. The spacious grounds were carefully manicured and had outdoor Stations of the Cross, numerous grottoes, statues and abundant colorful flowers. Coming up a rather steep incline to the main building, a sign stated, "Atonement is climbing to the top."

Checking at the information desk, we were advised a room would not be available until four o'clock but we could stash our packs in a side office. Then we went on a self-tour and found the snack bar and a marvelous book store to browse in. Seeing all these books made me keenly aware of how much I missed reading. Gene unsuccessfully attempted to find someone to drive him into Peekskill to buy groceries and fuel for our stove. It was then I asked the young man at the snack shop if he drove to work but he replied his mother chauffeured him each way. As we sat eating, he came over to us and said he believed his mother would be willing to help us. This son knew his mother! She graciously provided Gene with transportation to and from Peekskill.

While Gene was gone, we met Father Bosco who enthusiastically looks after the backpackers. He escorted us to our rooms, showed us the shower room and the laundry facilities and told us to be in the main dining room at six o'clock sharp for dinner. Teddy and I took advantage of all the facilities and reappeared transformed. The balanced scale in the ladies' room showed I now weighed one hundred ten pounds, approximately thirteen pounds less than when I started in Georgia.

The main dining room was huge and filled to capacity as a retreat was being held for lay people who work in different ministries, such as the prison ministry. The beautiful wall mural captivated me. Depicting the Last Supper, it portrayed Jesus standing, surrounded by His Apostles. Beneath were the words, "The One Bread Makes Us One Body Though Many in Number."

Bill, Lou, Gene, Teddy and I sat at a round table with our host, Father Bosco. As soon as a serving dish was empty, Father jumped up and had it refilled, until all of us were satiated. At the close of the meal, Father said the dining room was open all night for midnight snacks or juices, fruits and cereal.

The Franciscan Friars' hospitality was a beautiful example of welcoming strangers and making them feel at home and one in the spirit of God. No wonder their hospitality was a source of conversation all along the trail!

Teddy and I attended the evening service, commemorating the eight-hundredth anniversary of St. Francis' birth. A joyful celebration, my sister and I agreed it was a meaningful way for us to end our days together on the trail. In a few weeks she'd be leaving the United States to begin her missionary work in Guatemala, Central America.

August 4

After an unbelievable breakfast, we three went to wait for the bus, having purchased Teddy's ticket the previous day. All too quickly we were embracing each other farewell and

Teddy was on her way back to Greenwich Village in New York City. We would not see each other again for several years. However, Teddy continued with us as a TMIS—a team member in spirit.

We departed from Graymoor the same time as Englishman Bill and hiked together most of the day. The trail followed unpaved country roads a good portion of the way and each time a car drove past, a cloud of dust settled over us. The heat and humidity, added to the grit, made us especially thirsty. A man, caring for his flowers, provided us with cold water, as did a lady who scolded her geese, coaxing them away from us. Having broken them of the habit of chasing cars, she was still teaching them not to bite people.

Tomorrow we'd be watching for the home of the Giesekings, supposedly located alongside the trail around Holmes, New York. They were distant relatives of my Uncle Peter, and, although we had never met each other, Uncle Peter advised them we'd be passing through, and we were told to stop by.

Thirteen and a half miles later, we reached Fahnstock State Park. Too weary to even use the shower, I was asleep by eight o'clock.

August 5 - 18 miles

We stood at the edge of the road admiring a rustic log cabin, set on a knoll facing a mountain range, half-barrels of yellow and orange flowers placed about, and a circular swimming pool situated down a slope from the house. A huge St. Bernard charged towards us and Gene tightened his grip on his walking stick. This wasn't necessary, though, as the animal braked at the wire fence a few feet from us.

About a mile later, we reached the general store in Holmes, New York, and inquired where the Giesekings lived. A man, overhearing the lady tell us we'd have to backtrack, offered to drive us back after he learned we had already walked eighteen miles. He told us to wait while he went home to get his station wagon. To our delight, he deposited

114

us back at the picturesque log cabin, which had earlier totally captivated us. We had completely overlooked the mail box on the opposite side of the road. Replying to our knock, a voice called, "Who is it?" "Relatives from New York," I responded. How does one easily explain my mother's sister's husband's cousin's daughter?

Rosemary, my Uncle Peter's cousin's daughter, and Jerry, her husband, welcomed us royally and invited us to spend the night. Rosemary had a previous commitment but Jerry said he'd prepare our dinner, fresh trout. After we showered, they suggested we wear their swim suits and take advantage of the pool. Having never worn a bikini before, I laughed at my image of a scrawny body with a hiker's tan. Those parts of me that were daily exposed to the sun were golden brown, while all other parts were white. The pretty but skimpy suit bared lots of white! Gene looked comical, too, in oversized swim trunks, but the cool waters soothed our tired muscles and rejuvenated us for a delightful evening with our hosts.

August 6

A moist tongue, lapping my hand, awakened me at six o'clock. Opening my eyes, I was affectionately greeted good morning by Shenandoah. Smiling, I wondered how we could have been intimidated by this friendly animal. Looking over to where Gene slept, I caught sight of the mountains through our windows and eagerly arose.

Even though Rosemary had to leave early for her job in New York City, she had prepared us a breakfast of bacon, eggs, coffee, and English muffins with homemade preserves. She had also packed us a dozen fresh eggs, two venison pepperoni, home grown honey, ham and cheese sandwiches and peaches to go. After eating and taking pictures of this generous couple and their "storybook home," which they had built themselves from precut logs, we all left to go our separate ways, taking lasting memories with us.

Passing through Holmes a second time, we picked up our mail, a package and eight letters. One was a long letter from a group of our friends in Marriage Encounter, who, when gathered together for a Circle Meeting, had each added a few lines of encouragement and inspiration.

Road walking took us to the Ed Murrow State Park just in time for lunch before more hot road walking. A rare mid-afternoon nap off the road a few yards refreshed me, as I wasn't used to going to bed at eleven when hiking.

When our water ran out, I stopped at a house where a man invited me to step inside the cool foyer while he filled our canteens. At the Pawling Nature Sanctuary, the mosquitoes fiercely attacked us and out of desperation, I put on my flannel long sleeved shirt, long pants and kerchief, convinced it was better to roast than be chewed up.

August 7 Connecticut

At Wabetuck Pass a giant-sized wooden captain's chair called attention to the furniture store alongside the road and lured Gene to climb up into it to try it out. It dwarfed my Mountain Man, who appeared shrunken from lack of food. Once I stopped laughing, I snapped his picture, recording this comical moment.

Soaking my feet in a running brook, I was writing in my log when Whiskey Dave appeared. He was pressing hard, aiming to be at the Post Office by noon the next day. Pausing, he offered to get our mail, too, and leave it at the package store, well-known along the trail for giving a free beer to the through-hikers.

The big moment came as we stepped over a white line painted on a boulder, high on some ledges, with the words New York printed on one side and Connecticut on the other side. We were leaving the Middle States and entering New England. Embracing each other, we were overcome with emotion and began to cry. These Northern states had been seducing us for months. At last, we were here. We were filled with joy and expectancy, believing the ultimate was yet to come.

Mount Algo rudely introduced us to Connecticut and forced me to bend my stiff knees. Surveying its northern slope, a mass of jumbled, irregularly shaped boulders, Gene commented in his deep even voice, as we were deciding how to reach the white blazes, "Hmmmm, this looks interesting." Whenever he said that I knew I was in trouble.

Our day ended camping in Macedonia State Park.

August 8

Severe erosion made the trail over St. John's Ledges treacherous. Beginning to climb the ledges, we met two paid employees of the Appalachian Trail, presently supervising a special work crew from New Hampshire in the process of constructing a new and safer route. Due to the nature of the terrain, the task required highly skilled and technical workers. Blasting was delayed as we slowly worked our way down the critical descent. Safely reaching the bottom, we agreed that Mount Algo demanded more physical effort than the ledges. Fortunately, that was the next planned reroute.

The next five miles were all flat and a blessed relief after the strain of our earlier challenge. Walking parallel to the Housatonic River, between colossal pine trees, I felt an intimate sense of place, which was incomprehensible to me at the time.

As we crossed the Housatonic Bridge, the first store was the package store. A man came running out, calling us by our first names. He had our envelope (with checks) sent by our daughter. Dave had reached the Post Office in time. The clerk told us to hurry across the street to the general store as they would close in ten minutes, asking us to return later to sign the register. As I selected groceries for supper and breakfast, Gene arranged for the last motel room, vacant because of a cancellation only moments before. Then he went back to sign the register, get his free beer, a free Sprite for me and a bottle of New York State white wine, a treat to ourselves.

We had hiked seventy-one miles in the last four days!

August 9

Our end room at the Bonnie Brook Motel had windows on three sides providing us with ample fresh air. The luxury of another warm shower and a breakfast of all fresh fruits began our day. Before leaving, Gene phoned his cousin, Ray, whom he hadn't seen in thirty years, and arranged to meet him and Ray's mother in Dalton, Massachusetts, approximately one hundred-twenty miles north of where we were.

The morning was sunny and warm and the trail wound gently through wooded areas It would have been a perfect day except for the fact that me left jaw throbbed incessantly. The extra strength Tylenol helped my knees more than my mouth and the constant pain distracted me.

Entering a pine forest, raining pine needles, we chose this place to have our dinner and were relaxing when a father and his two teenage sons came along. From Morristown, New Jersey, they were hiking the trail through Connecticut and Massachusetts. This was their second attempt as they had to abort their first trip early in the summer when the father fell on Cobble Mountain, injuring himself.

Later on, having passed over several ski slopes, we walked through a campground. As we pumped water into our canteens, I heard a loud ding-a-ling and instantly knew what that sound meant from my childhood days—the Good Humor Ice Cream man. I cried, "Drop everything and hurry!" Like two children, we excitedly ran up the hill to hail the ice cream truck and ordered two ice creams each. Energized, we hiked into dusk, stopping when it became dark. Together, we shared the last of our wine and it helped to soothe my aching jaw.

August 10

A solo southbound hiker, with legs as sturdy as tree trunks, met us early in the morning. Having started at Katahdin, she exhibited excellent physical conditioning.

Exchanging trail tips, we learned there was a coffee shop, "The Village," at Route #7, and at once decided to do the ten miles farther and have our lunch there.

After having hiked through three drought plagued states, we rejoiced as beautifully wooded Dean Ravine flaunted its running brook. The sight and sound and taste of it truly excited us. We no longer took water for granted.

Almost to Route #7, we met a perspiring college football player, having the physique of a running back, trying to catch up to the young woman we had passed earlier. After we answered his question concerning her whereabouts, he remarked that they had spent the previous night together and that he wished to get to know her better. Being only a weekend hiker, hiking to stay in shape for the up and coming football season, we wondered if he ever succeeded, as it was obvious he was having trouble maintaining her pace.

At the coffee shop, my lunch consisted of roast beef on rye, pickled beets, strawberry milkshake, coffee, apple pie a la mode and a huge orange juice. Gene had two hamburgers, french fries, a milkshake and pumpkin pie with two ice creams. As we were leaving, a man from the Appalachian Trail Conference introduced himself and we chatted awhile. Shortly after, as we walked along the road, a truck pulled over and a couple stopped to talk with us, giving us raisins, and sharing experiences from their through-hike in 1975.

The afternoon's walk took us through tall purple meadowrue, growing in profusion along the Housatonic River, and by homes built in 1876. Simple in structure and immaculate, as if just newly painted, their shuttered windows had sparkling panes and fluffy white curtains. Colorful flowers decorated the walkways. I had the feeling the interiors were as spotless and uncluttered as the exteriors. Stopping in front of a barn red home, which especially appealed to Gene, we were about to ask permission to photograph it when we noticed a full pail of apples set alongside the white picket fence with the sign, "Hikers, Welcome to Sugar Hill, help yourselves, come back next year." Taking pictures, we ate three apples and stashed several more into our packs.

Climbing over one more mountain, Mount Prospect, we reached Salisbury, Connecticut, about seven-thirty. The Langleys, friends of my aunt, lived on Upper Cobble Road close to the trail and, although we had never met before, Helen and Jim welcomed us warmly. While we showered, Helen prepared us a supper, and after we ate, she told me to call my aunt in Long Island. A retired doctor, my Aunt Peg's first question was, "What condition did you two arrive in?" Laughing, I told her the truth, "Hot, dirty, tired and hungry." Dad then surprised us with a call, since Aunt Peg called him to update him on our whereabouts. While we visited, Helen threw our soiled clothes into the washer and dryer.

Turning in at eleven, we had the whole upstairs to ourselves and slept in a huge soft bed with lots of fresh air coming through the windows.

August 11 Massachusetts

The aroma of bacon awakened me. Up at dawn, Gene was already outside on the patio, enjoying the quiet and a cup of freshly brewed coffee.

After a leisurely breakfast, Jim drove us into Salisbury where Gene purchased needed socks while I shopped for fresh produce. We repacked our packs, photographed our newest friends and benefactors, Jim and Helen, and were on the trail by ten o'clock, a rather late start for such a blistering day. The two miles up to the Lions Head were sweltering and we paused to rest and eat some pears and grapes. No matter how much we ate, it seemed we were always hungry.

The climb up Bear Mountain was steep but manageable as there were numerous places to grab onto. Besides, the Tylenol was helping my knees to bend without causing me to groan.

Lunching in Sage Ravine, where there was an occasional cool breeze, we marvelled at all the crystal clear, fast running waters. Before long, we crossed into Massachusetts, the eleventh state along our journey. Although excellent swimming holes tempted us, we knew we should keep moving, having gotten such a late start.

Walking along open cliffs to the summit of Race Mountain, we found ourselves heading directly into a blackened sky and close to colliding with an imminent storm. Cool winds brushed our hot faces and mega-sized rain drops sprinkled us. Behind us, the mountains stood silhouetted against a peach-colored sky and we hurried along, anxious to get below the treeline.

Near the base of Mount Everett, we hastily erected our tent, only seconds before the rains came in torrents. We managed to keep the inside of our tent dry but had to forego supper.

I awoke once during the night with my tooth aching, but other than that, we slept soundly.

August 12

Gene's deep voice called, "Coffee is ready. It looks as though the sun will shine." Since everything was still dripping wet, he served us breakfast in the tent.

Gene was dressed in his fleece-lined Mountain Man shirt and shorts, and it was a joy for me to observe his lean, muscular body ascending Mount Everett. His muscles moved rhythmically as he advanced gracefully. Even though the rocks were wet, they were not slippery. The view from the top reminded us of our Great Smoky Mountains in Tennessee with billows of mist arising from the mountains.

At Jug End, we took several pictures before scrambling down ledges to a graveled highway. Finding a good piped spring, we decided to have a hot lunch before beginning six miles of road walking.

Along the way, we met a southbound hiker and I asked him his feelings about the White Mountains in New Hampshire. With a glint in his eyes, he answered, "They are not totally unyielding, but they do cut one's hiking time in half."

121

After the road walking, we hiked four more miles in the woods, ending on East Mountain. Our feet stung from the miles on the pavement and we decided to stop once we found water, even though we had only made fourteen and one-half miles.

August 13

Ledges, road walking, marshy areas and pleasing woods filled our morning. Stopping at Benedict Pond in Beartown State Forest, I perched on a huge rock to write and soaked my feet in the cool waters while Gene prepared our food. A strong breeze blew through the slender birch and spruce trees, coaxing the water to lap the shoreline. The whole scene gave us but an inkling of what Maine had to offer.

Later in the afternoon, we walked through a pine forest denuded by a blight. The trees were stark skeletons, standing at attention, amidst mounds of brown needles, while sporadic patches of green ferns, in dramatic contrast, gave hope for new life.

Coming off Mt. Wilcox, we came into the peaceful valley of Tyringham, comprised of farmlands and a tiny township. After three miles of road walking, we passed Goose Pond, encircled by summer and winter homes. Two and a half miles farther, we reentered the woods, a relief to our feet, and soon after I put up the tent by myself while Gene backtracked for water.

After an eighteen-and-a-half-mile day, we were ready to crawl into our sleeping bags without any fanfare.

August 14

We crossed over the Massachusetts Turnpike about ten o'clock in the morning and tried without luck to purchase a cup of real coffee at the motel we passed. The lady explained it was reserved for those patronizing the motel.

Disappointed, we realized that this was the only time someone refused a request.

Descending from the first summit of Becket Mountain, we walked through an impressive grove of beech trees before ascending the second summit of Becket Mountain.

Finerty Pond became our lunch stop and the warmth of noontime sunshine made us feel good. This confirmed we were getting farther north.

August 15

On the walk into the town of Dalton, Massachusetts, I took a picture of Gene posed beside a fire hydrant manufactured by U. S. Pipe and Valve Company, the company which gave him his six-months leave of absence after twenty-two years of service. This was one of the few times since beginning our hike that he spoke about his work.

The cement sidewalks caused Gene's foot to hurt more than usual and he gladly sat down in front of the Post Office while I went in to pick up our parcel and ask directions to the community center. Gene frowned and groaned when he learned the community center was one-half mile away. Overhearing our comments, Jack McKenna, who was standing close by, spontaneously offered his assistance. Handing Gene his newspaper, he said, "Here, you read this while I drive your partner to the center to check out the accommodations." Beaming and without any hesitation, I hopped into his Volkswagen and off we drove. Looking incredulous, Gene gratefully remained seated.

The gentleman in charge at the center showed us a spacious room about twenty feet by thirty feet, with thick mats to put our sleeping bags on and "his" and "her" showers downstairs, with towels provided. A pay telephone hung accessible in the hallway. All this free luxury was the town's way of welcoming through-hikers.

Across the street was a restaurant aptly named "Best Restaurant" and two blocks farther was a food store. Jack stopped at the store, directing me to go in and see if it had what we might need. Laughing, I told him, "Yes, it has ice cream, bread and fresh fruits, plus."

Twenty minutes later, Jack helped Gene jam our packs and walking sticks into the backseat of his beetle. Sitting in Gene's lap up front, my head bumping the roof, we headed back to the community center. With the car unloaded, Jack produced two brand new T-shirts from the backseat and benevolently bestowed these upon Gene, who happily accepted this man's gift. The shirt Gene was wearing had two conspicuous holes where his pack straps rubbed. Many times we have reflected on our brief encounter with Jack, whose spirit of brotherhood added a touch of wonder to our arrival in Dalton, Massachusetts.

Later in the afternoon, Gene's Aunt Ada and Cousin Ray arrived from Schenectady, New York. Our reunion included dinner at Bonanza's. Waiting in line, we all noted with mirth the disparity in appearances—the lady ahead of me in her sheer stockings and slender high heels and me in my heavy wool socks and well-worn Danner boots. Gene, handsome in his new shirt, glowed with his good fortune.

This unforgettable day ended when, brushing my teeth, I found to my dismay half my molar had broken off, leaving a gaping hole.

August 16

The second dentist I called suggested going to the dental resident at the Berkshire Medical Center, open seven days a week. Liking the idea of seeing someone immediately, I called Paul, my brother's friend who lived in the heart of New York City but who escaped to Cheshire, Massachusetts, on weekends. Within the hour I was sitting in the dentist's chair, a root canal in progress. An X-ray showed my broken tooth was abscessed and the nerve dead. Since the nurses were out on strike, Paul assisted the dentist, operating the suction machine and giving me moral support. One and a half hours later, I gratefully climbed out of the dentist's chair, a temporary patch protecting the remains of my tooth.

Months later, after we were home, a bill came for twenty-five dollars!

Picking up Gene and our packs, Paul drove us to his summer residence where an afternoon of volley ball followed. Gene joined Paul and his friends, who played hard to win and not simply for fun, but his boots hindered him. I was content to work in the garden with a young neighbor, June, pulling weeds and cultivating around the plants. Later Paul invited us to join him and his friends — Joyce, Misha and Luchia and their sixteen-year-old son, Ralph — for the son's birthday celebration at Shuy's Japanese restaurant. The food, beautifully served and a picture to behold, made it also a visual eating experience.

All too soon, Paul bid us goodbye and we squeezed into Misha's low slung sports car and had another fast ride. Wow! Earlier, driving with Paul, the trees had been a green blur and I felt as if we were flying. Returning with Misha, though, even Gene said, "Wow!" At Gene's request, they took us back to the community center so we could continue where we left off. I went straight to bed, as by now my jaw was throbbing and I felt miserable. A Phenerphen #3 did not give me any relief, so after pacing the floor a while, I took two extra strength Tylenol and finally slept.

August 17

At the Best Restaurant by six, we were underway while it was still gray out. The cold, crisp air made us feel vibrant and we moved at a sprightly pace. The miles between Dalton and Cheshire were easy and most pleasant. The intriguing cloud formations helped to distract me from thinking about my sore jaw.

In Cheshire, the trail crossed right in front of the Post Office. This would have been an ideal mail drop had we known about it. Farther along, we picked up some cold cuts, milk and yogurt and, upon leaving town, went off the road into a field of wildflowers and had our lunch and a siesta.

The afternoon sun felt warm and soothing to us, proof that fall was upon us.

Later on, as we walked along a country road, Lori's father stopped his station wagon and offered to take our packs to Mt. Greylock for us. He had Lori's and Peter's, two through-hikers, and would be driving the road up to the summit. The offer tempted us but we declined, feeling we'd be giving up our independence.

At seven p.m., weary and cold after seventeen miles of hiking and more aware that independence demands a price, we sighted Bascom Lodge—a low sprawling building on the very summit. The lodge, constructed by the Civilian Conservation Corps during the Depression, was made of stone and logs, having wide beams and two enormous fireplaces downstairs with dormitory style rooms upstairs.

This night the Lord revealed all His glory and majesty in the sky—a truly spectacular sunset flooded the heavens with electrifying reds, oranges and golds, creating a flaming backdrop for the Catskills and Adirondack Mountains in New York, the Green Mountains in Vermont and the Berkshires in Massachusetts, all seen from this high place.

A hot shower helped me to warm up but I refrained from washing my hair, and instead put on the turtleneck sweater Paul had loaned us. The irony of it all made me laugh—lots of hot running water and it was too cold to take full advantage of it.

A roaring fire in the fireplace warmed us until we retired. Although the five single beds in our room were all empty, Gene invited me to share his bed and I happily jumped in. Snuggled up next to my Mountain Man, I could enjoy the warmth radiating from his body. Feeling all his ribs, though, alarmed me; he was getting too thin, especially when he needed a layer of fat to help keep him warm in these final days.

August 18 Vermont

The cold morning convinced us it was time to request warm clothing be sent from home. Since no sounds were emitting from the kitchen, we assumed the cook had not arrived and we remained in our cozy bed with a clear conscience. About seven-thirty, a few pots rattled and Gene leaped out of bed, soon to return with steaming coffee.

We each enjoyed a double breakfast in the dining room where flowering baskets hung from the wooden beams and flowering plants stood on the sills of the large windows that brought the outside in. Fortified, we stepped out into the glorious sunshine and hiked briskly to keep warm on this cold morning. Before long, exertion heated us and we had to stop and shed a layer of clothing.

Reaching the town of North Adams near three o'clock, we decided to have our dinner at a Burger King located a half-mile off the trail. Afterwards we retraced our steps and, having crossed over the Hoosic River via a footbridge, walked alongside Sherman Brook. The trail then climbed steeply taking us to an open ridge. Along here, we met a mother and her sixteen-year-old son, Peter, hiking together. Heading to Jug End, he exhibited pride to be hiking with his mother. I felt happy for her.

At six o'clock we crossed the state line entering the gentle state of Vermont, where the Long Trail and the Appalachian Trail are one and the same for ninety-seven miles.

By eight we were ready to call it a day and I donned Paul's sweater and my wool cap.

August 19

Orange spotted touch-me-nots and purple stemmed asters grew alongside the brook where we stopped to eat. The sun warmed the back of my neck and a feeling of gratitude for "being" welled up within me. All life is a gift to be cherished.

Stone and log steps made the descent of Harmon Hill, two thousand three hundred feet down, easy. We were impressed by this masterpiece of trail engineering and grateful for all the hard work it took to implement.

Twelve hours and seventeen miles after starting out, we reached the Milville Nauheim Shelter and decided to sleep in it. This would be our first time to sleep in a shelter since the murders in Pearisburg. As we were getting settled, a solo hiker arrived. Kathy, whom we had last seen the day previous to our departure from Pearisburg, was no longer a chubby girl but, instead, a streamlined, pretty young woman. The transition confirmed another benefit of hiking the trail.

August 20

'We need to pick the right time to rest so that we can continue.'

Rocks and roots challenged us all day. Only the wooden footways, constructed to cross the swampy areas, gave us an occasional respite. When darkness approached, we simply set up our tent alongside the trail. Having travelled over fifteen miles, our feet were too weary to try to make it to the shelter, but that was okay as we had made our quota of necessary miles.

August 21

Determined to do a twenty-mile day, we arose at daybreak and were on our way by seven. Passing the lean-to, we saw a couple and their five young children putting on their packs. It gave us a warm feeling to see a family and their dog in such a setting. We also knew we had made the right decision last night.

Miles of narrow wooden walkways (over two hundred), protected the marshy areas leading to Stratton Pond, which reflected Stratton Mountain. At the far end of the pond, beavers had built their house.

Missing the new reroute, we walked through a luxuriant but poorly marked area. Bark off the birch trees was strewn about like ribbons. A trillium boasted a single red berry in the center of its three leaves. This scarlet seed signified the end of the flowering cycle, but held the promise of a new beginning. In the early part of our journey, the flowering trilliums thrilled us and we photographed them many times. I was deeply touched by seeing this trillium in a different phase of its cycle of life, as it was still very beautiful.

Eighteen miles later, we decided to call it a day. For supper each of us devoured four packages of instant oatmeal and loved every spoonful. This episode would have made a convincing Quaker Oats commercial. Our feet stung and we were simply grateful to unlace our boots and lie down.

August 22

While walking to Route #11, white baneberry, "doll's eyes," caught my attention. Wet with dew, they appeared to be shedding tears and I wished to photograph them, but, my Mountain Man was too hungry and in too big a hurry to reach Manchester. At the moment, picture-taking did not interest him in the least.

Standing alongside the highway, Gene confidently stuck out his thumb and told me to do likewise. Feeling embarrassed, I hesitantly began my first hitchhiking experience. The fourth car stopped and a friendly, attractive woman in her forties offered to drive us to Manchester and back again in three hours, as she was going to the beauty shop and grocery store. She thoughtfully suggested we leave our packs in the car, which we did.

When we stopped at Friendly's for breakfast, people stared at us with curiosity. It's strange but I never felt different until we went into a town. I held my head high and responded to their scrutiny with a smile.

The Health Food Store was our second stop, where we bought nuts, dried fruits and a honey bear, before going to the Food Mart for our main staples. Early in our hike, we learned that freeze-dried foods did not provide the calories we needed and did not sustain us, but we did discover that pasta, rice, instant milk and cheese gave us time-released energy. Once, we met a weekend hiker heading in the opposite direction. Seeing we had hiked from Georgia, he wanted instant answers, saying, "Give it to me fast. What are the three main foods?" Gene and I simultaneously blurted out different responses; his, "water, noodles, cheese," and mine, "pasta, rice, instant milk, cereal and ..." He hurried on, evidently satisfied, before I could mention ice cream.

We were back at the car at the designated time, but Patsy had not yet arrived. Gene went into the Carol Reed Ski Shop and came out all smiles and told me to go in and select a wool sweater, whereupon I chose a soft gray Shetland wool in size thirty-six that fit perfectly. When Patsy arrived, she drove us to the gas station for fuel and back to the trail where Gene took a picture of us standing together by the Appalachian Trail sign. It would show two smiling women at different ends of the spectrum — stylishness and simplicity.

Patsy offered us the key to her summer home in Ludlow, but we declined after learning it was eleven miles off the trail. Then she asked if we needed anything she had. What impressed us most of all, though, was learning that her growth resulted from twelve years in Alcoholics Anonymous and graduating from college the previous year with a degree in social work. This woman's courage and kindness affected us. Afterwards, Gene and I talked about how some people's lives touch ours, ever so briefly, leaving an imprint to last a lifetime.

With heavy loads and a bag of fruit in hand, we began the steep ascent up Bromley Mountain. Halfway up we met a young woman hiking south and stopped to talk with her and to share our fruit. Near the summit, the trail went up the center of the ski slope. Turning around, I tried to imagine what it would be like to ski into such beauty. On top a wooden observation tower gave us an excellent view of the cold, gray, dramatic scene showing peaks in five states.

This evening a spruce forest provided us with a campsite. Sitting on a rock in a clearing away from our site, I tried to capture the last rays of light in order to write in my journal. Minutes later, looking up, everything appeared black in the forest, but I could sense all the wonders hidden within. The woods are like people; their depths hold richness and diversity, waiting to be discovered.

August 23

It was Sunday, the Lord's Day, and the Green Mountains in all their freshness felt sacred to me. We climbed Styles Peak and on the summit took off our packs and sat in the sunlight to absorb the beauty we were a part of. I wished Teddy, Mary, Barry, Mom and Dad, and everyone I felt close to could be up here with us to experience it together. We had to force ourselves to leave. We rested briefly on Peru Peak amidst the pines (no view here) before hiking to Griffith Lake.

Sitting on Bakers Peak in the middle of the afternoon, a tapestry of farmlands was seen in Otter Creek Valley far below. Mountains, emerald in the sunlight, could be seen in most directions.

Back in the woods, we were sprinkled by a brief sun shower before we reached Little Rock Pond, where we paid a fee to the lady caretaker in residence to use a platform site for the night. Here a solar system outhouse, the first we had seen, was surprisingly fresh smelling.

August 24

'New life is everywhere. If we stop, look and listen, we can see our own place in life! I love you!'

Something wonderful happened within me today! Walking through a rich pine forest, we were fascinated by all the saplings growing beneath the tall pines, wedged so tightly together that they appeared attached. The earth, nourishing this new generation, was black and fertile and moist. I touched these healthy young pines; their needles, soft and silky, were pliable in my hands, their fragrance fresh and pleasing like a newborn. A huge old tree, broken near its roots, lay nearby, slowly decaying. In the process of decomposition, this once stately tree was feeding new life, as green shoots sprouted from its very side. It was still serving an important purpose.

Pondering on the cycle of life, all at once, my present place in this cycle became excitingly clear to me. I am one of the tall pines, mature, reaching upward to the sun, forever becoming — fulfilling God's plan. The tiny trees are my children; they will grow and survive and attain completeness, depending on the soil I help provide and also on the outside forces, the uncontrollable elements. As I have experienced on this journey, symbolic of my journey through life, the elements are gentle as well as fierce, conducive to growth as well as to destruction. It is up to me to provide rich soil — love — not only for my children, but for all children, young and old. How I live my life, how I love, how I reach out to others, how I respond, affects countless other human beings. This makes my life, to the day I die, significant. My legacy to this world's people is vital. How strange, I do not feel this responsibility is a burden, but rather a privilege, a joy to understand. Seemingly free of responsibility all these months, I had discovered I am never totally free of responsibility.

That evening, sitting in the grass on Beacon Hill and meditating, I felt in exquisite harmony with God, all His people and with myself.

August 25

Mist floated in as I sipped my coffee. A single purple thistle bloomed nearby, marking this unforgettable place.

Our morning break was taken by a rushing brook, and even though it was cool, we put our feet into a frothy whirlpool until they turned numb. The weather was overcast and before lunchtime a light drizzle fell.

We climbed steadily over a rugged trail that took us through an evergreen tree farm and over Little Killington. Inspecting Tamarack Shelter, we saw the biggest rabbit I've ever seen. The caretaker at Little Rock Pond told us the porcupines were a real problem here. Chicken wire had been nailed around the bottom of the shelter to deter the porcupines from chewing the wood.

The summit of Killington Peak was completely concealed by fog and we kept moving. About five we reached Pico Peak and only then did it begin to clear.

The Long Trail Inn on Route 4 wouldn't cash our check and we had to hike up the side of Deer Leap Mountain before finding a soft, lumpy spot to set up our tent.

August 26

The trail, skirting Kent Lake, passed close to Mountain Meadows Lodge, and we arrived just in time to stop for breakfast. Appearing totally different with her long dark hair combed loose, Jan was sitting at the table we were directed to. She is the girl we met as we climbed Mount Bromley. After eating, Jan volunteered to drive Gene into Killington, three miles round trip, to pick up our mail and the package from Mary, which contained a pair of wool slacks, new red rain jacket and homemade granola.

Upon his return, Gene surprised me by suggesting we spend the day at Mountain Meadows and rest. The price was right, six-fifty for board and breakfast. Canoeing on Kent Lake, I felt like a kid playing hookey. I did that once in the second grade and loved every minute, as I did today. Gliding around an inlet, we watched a blue heron take off in flight. Ascending in slow motion, this huge bird exhibited gracefulness. The lake mirrored the surrounding mountain, a phenomenon that never ceased to intrigue me. Paddling through these mountains, we photographed unusual water flowers, agreeing that this change of pace was good for us.

We declined Jan's invitation to accompany her and her friend, Peter, to dinner and summer theater to see *Fiddler on the Roof*, as we wished to canoe at dusk and retire early.

August 27

Joined by Jan and Peter, our day began with an "all you can eat breakfast" and stimulating conversation. Before departing, we took their picture in front of the lodge and left, feeling a warm glow from our time spent here and with these people. Breezy, it was fairly cool and it was reassuring to me to have my warm clothing tucked inside my pack, making it heavier but still manageable.

As we sat by a brook to snack, Whiskey Dave came along. Looking rested after a week off the trail, spent with his grandmother, he sported a new pack frame and pack belt and repaired boots. We gave him Bill and Dave's message to meet them in Hanover, New Hampshire, as they planned on partying all the way to the "Big K."

In the evening, the trail took us down a country road along which we met a lady outside her home. When we stopped to talk, she told us that years ago her mother had given Grandma Gatewood an inexpensive watch when she passed by here on one of her through hikes. It meant something to me to know that Grandma Gateway, who hiked the entire trail twice, walked down this very same road.

The sign read, "No Trapping, Fishing, Hunting." Since we had no intentions of doing these things, we felt comfortable with setting up our tent on top of a hill, out of sight.

August 28

'Beauty is everywhere. All we need to do is look. I love you.'

Today's joys were special gifts from the Lord and Farmer Johnson. The latter allowed the through-hikers to hike on his property, instead of walking six miles on macadam roads. Mr. Johnson had even made his own signs directing the hikers across the rolling hills of his farmlands.

Walking in dew-drenched grass, we discovered delicate spider webs dangling from tree branches. These intricate masterpieces trapped droplets of moisture that sparkled like jewels. Thrilled, we slipped out of our packs and carefully photographed our finds. One web shattered as we gingerly moved the branch to better captivate the light, sending a pang of sadness through me. Later, we noticed other kinds of webs suspended in the tall grass. Opaque, they resembled white silk cloth.

At the end of Farmer Johnson's property, we crossed an old wooden bridge. To the right stood a stately dead tree decorated with numerous spider webs — each a work of art. Our picture of this aged tree is one of my favorites.

We were enthralled by the simplicity and complexity of life that this tree symbolized.

August 29 New Hampshire

Crossing over the Connecticut River, we walked into Hanover, New Hampshire, at seemingly the same time as droves of college students. They were swarming like bees. We chose to forgo the Foley Fraternity House and the promised "wild time" and, instead, headed for the laundromat and food store. Chores completed, we sat on the green in the center of the Dartmouth complex and had lunch. Englishman Bill, Whiskey Dave, and Dave, accompanied by his new friend, Tashia, all stopped by to talk with us before we put our packs on and hiked out of town.

August 30

Feeling ultra feminine and sensual, I expressed my sexual desire for my husband. When he did not respond as I anticipated, a loneliness filled me. My frustration was slowly released, though, working my way up the flat rocks to the cap of Mount Smarts. The way up was steep, especially the last mile. I could feel the perspiration rolling down my face and dripping off the hairs on the back of my neck. My T-shirt became soaked and the thought occurred to me that the last time I was this wet with sweat was in the final stages of labor with our son. Ultimately, the physical demands of this mountain effectively tamed my sexual drive.

An open shelter, perched on the very top, was battened down by two cables. Dense fog, rising from below, prevented us from seeing anything, except in our immediate area. We were standing on the tip of an iceberg in a sea of white.

Farther along, we chose to bypass a crude cabin, as we felt it would be used by the three fellows if they made their planned twenty-one miles. Instead, we descended and erected our tent alongside a brook, eating as darkness set in.

Our day ended as Gene rubbed my sore feet and I massaged his tired back.

August 31

Rejuvenated by sound sleep, our dawn began with a "love feast." My Mountain Man's coarse beard felt marvelous as he kissed and caressed me, and we lovingly journeyed to the summit together and lingered there, without ever leaving our tent. When we finally did emerge, we faced the new day with freshness and vigor.

Walking along the woods roads, we passed old homes, some dating back to the Revolutionary War days, prominently displaying the American flag. Seeing the Stars and Stripes stirred feelings of patriotism and pride deep within us and we talked about freedom. Since the first day on the trail, we experienced freedom to a degree never known by us before and we exulted in it.

The next mountain, Mount Cube, proved to be different. It's granite-type cube shaped rocks were easy to scramble up and not at all slippery. We stopped to put on our wool shirts and hats close to the summit but removed them halfway down the other side. It was then we discovered plastic tubing extending from the maple trees, snaking its way down the mountainside. This modern way of collecting syrup was not at all like the picturesque method I had seen in books—a hollow tube drilled into a tree with a pail hanging off the end of it, with men in colorful plaid shirts checking on their contents.

Towards evening the mosquitoes became thick and intolerable, and, even though it was humid, I resorted to long sleeves and pants. Walking along the Old Cohos Road, originally laid out in 1768, I felt the lives of people, who lived years ago, touch mine in an almost tangible way as we enjoyed the fruits of their labor—the road.

This night we camped on private property.

September 1

'The gentle slopes are easy to traverse, but the difficult ones are hard to get to know! I love you.'

All morning we hiked briskly as autumn was in the air and we were eager to master Mount Moosilauke. Because of its fragile ecological state, no camping is permitted, and our goal was to be on the other side by nightfall. The five-thousand-foot ascent up Moosilauke, begun after lunching at its base, was pleasant work. Nearing the apex, we stopped to quickly change into warm dry clothes as the weather had turned cold, windy and foggy. The pine trees, lining either side of the last mile, shed large drops of water as we brushed past them. The last one-tenth mile to the sign marking the summit is not part of the Appalachian Trail but we went up in error, missing the white blaze. Gene's glasses clouded over, so I read the sign aloud for us. One sign stated a Mr. Woodworth donated the summit to Dartmouth in 1907. Grateful, we stood on the very pinnacle, a curtain of mist veiling our surroundings. Gene was not disappointed, though. Simply being there satisfied him. In retrospect, he loved this mountain best of all.

The trail down seemed more up at first and my energy began to wane. Gene said, "We'll stop as soon as we get down a little and out of this wind." The way down became progressively more difficult and then it began to rain. We kept going down, neglecting the rest period, in our earnestness to complete our descent before darkness set in.

We began hearing rushing waters and found ourselves hiking beside a cascade. The slick rocks and roots were hazardous to travel over, especially in the deepening dusk. The situation grew intense. My feet did not obey my brain's commands and went their own careless way. My knees grew stiffer from all the dampness. My pace slowed and I felt confused and uncertain. Gene realized the seriousness of our predicament. With approximately one-and-a-half miles to the bottom, he decided we must stop, judging it too risky not to. For the first time, hypothermia threatened. Pausing, Gene discerned a faint path to the right. About ten feet back, there was a tiny semi-level clearing.

The Lord again met our need and Gene again demonstrated his skills as a fearless Mountain Man and as a leader. Drifting off to sleep, I thought of this man God made for me to love. I need this man because I love him completely. How blessed I am!

September 2

'To radiate calmness, I must be calm! I love you.'

In the early morning sunlight, the cascade on our left was truly a masterpiece of the Lord's. The trail bordering these tumbling waters was treacherous with its slippery rocks, roots and steps. The steps, approximately two feet long wooden triangular shapes, were bolted into the slanted sheets of rock. Slowly and painfully, I worked my way down, my right arm aching from hanging onto the iron rails available in several places and from bracing myself on my walking stick. My stiff knees simply didn't want to bend sufficiently. The candid picture Gene took of me on these steps shows taut leg muscles and a strained look of concentration on my face.

The sign at the end of the descent read, "This trail is extremely rough. If you lack experience, please use another trail. Take special care at the cascades to avoid tragic results." Gene grinned at me and declared, "I guess we are considered experienced."

At the road in Kinsman's Notch, Gene stuck out his thumb. The second vehicle, a pickup, drove us six miles into Woodstock, which was one of our planned mail drops. Besides that, we were down to our last bank check and needed to arrange to have money sent. Up to this point, our hike had cost two thousand four hundred fifty dollars, proving our pre-hike calculations to be inaccurate, as two thousand dollars was to have covered our whole trip.

To our surprise, the bank teller didn't want to cash our fifty-dollar check. Until now, there never was a problem in a bank. How disappointing it was to be in a town and have only forty-nine cents in cash. We called our bank in Tennessee to request them to wire money to us, and they promised it would be there the next morning. Persistent, we pleaded our case, and finally the teller broke the bank rule and cashed our check. Her courtesy enabled us to eat dinner at The Lantern, buy fruit and eggs, do our laundry, splurge on a bottle of white wine and stay in a rooming house.

September 3

Standing alongside Route 112, we smiled and Gene put out his thumb. Twenty minutes and numerous cars later, Gene said, "If we don't get a ride in ten more minutes, I'll go to the gas station and see if I can pay a fellow to drive us back to the trail." With that, a car screeched to a halt and Mary, the lady I met in the laundromat last evening, called to us. She and her husband, Bob, offered to help us and managed to fit our packs and Gene into the backseat and me up front with them. Their trunk was filled with their luggage as they were on a motor trip through the New England states. Bob wanted to treat us to breakfast but we declined as already we had eaten twice while waiting for our money to arrive. Returning to Kinsman's Notch, we instead took time to show them the trail entrance, the blazes, our profile maps of the White Mountains and answer their questions.

Awed by the fact that we had travelled from Georgia to New Hampshire by following white blazes, they said they had difficulty just finding their car in the parking lot in New Jersey, their home state. After Gene took a picture of Bob, Mary and me, we parted, uplifted because of our brief encounter with these caring people.

The terrain immediately took us up a steep ascent and then it was a continuous succession of ups and downs with rocks and roots to contend with all along the way. We met a couple of southbound hikers, sprawled out alongside the trail, resting. The older of the two spoke of feeling discouraged by the ruggedness of this section.

By six o'clock dusk was settling in and we quickly selected a tent site not far from Eliza Shelter and a small stream.

September 4

'Some days are very difficult, but a smile will always save the day!'

This day I almost met my Waterloo! Only my Mountain Man's love and constant help, pushing and pulling me in the seemingly impossible places, kept me going. In several areas a sharp five-foot drop in the trail gradient appeared to be an insurmountable obstacle. With no place to put my feet, I was ready to concede defeat and to retreat, but Gene never considered giving up. He only believed in retreating to regroup — to plan a different approach. He jammed his walking stick against the vertical rock so I could step up onto it and stretch out and grab an exposed tree root. While I hung on, he moved the stick up and I stepped up a little higher and in this manner slowly worked my way up. With extreme patience and strength on Gene's part and stubbornness on mine, we progressed upward. At last, we were on the top of South Kinsman, and we blissfully walked on grass in blue skies and sunshine and silence.

Farther along, the rippling waters of Kinsman Pond sparkled in the sunlight. Stopping for lunch, we figured it had taken us four and one-half hours to cover four miles. At this rate, I wondered aloud if we would ever reach Katahdin. Gene wisely advised me to stop thinking of miles and dwell on the beauty. But I still thought about the miles.

The hike down was fairly easy but slow in places. Stopping at Lonesome Lake Hut, we spoke with Randy, the chef and all-around man. According to him, the huts mainly catered to the weekend and short-term hikers who knew what day they would arrive. Reservations were required to stay at one of the seven huts forming a chain over fifty miles of ridge trails. After today, we had no idea how long it would take us to travel over these mountain ranges.

This night we camped in an "off limits" state park. All our unorthodox maneuvers left us physically exhausted and not overly concerned about rules.

September 5

Awakening, I thought it was still dark out, but it was only my wool hat pulled down over my eyes. By six-thirty, we could hear people's voices and knew the labor day weekend was underway.

Coming to the entrance of the Franconia Range by 8:30, we began climbing Mount Liberty on the Liberty Spring Trail, also the Appalachian Trail. We hiked straight up — slowly, steadily, without pausing — going from four hundred feet to four thousand. Along the way, a group of young men hurried past me five different times, but each time they had to stop and catch their breath for their next spurt. One hiker actually became ill with stomach cramps. Two and a half miles and several hours later, we arrived simultaneously at Liberty Spring Campsite. One of these men, panting and sweating, queried, "Lady, don't you ever get tired?" What a compliment! What a misconception! At this point, I felt I could climb anything as long as there was a place to plant my feet. The secret, of course, learned early in our journey, was to travel at one's own pace, even if it meant being last most of the time.

The afternoon was spent above the timberline, proceeding over Little Mt. Haystack, Mt. Lincoln and Mt. Lafayette, being careful to stay within the confines of the narrow path, frequently lined on either side with a low stone wall, an attempt to prevent further erosion from heavy boots. The wealth of alpine vegetation needed protection!

No wonder I had no preconceived mental image of the White Mountains. I never could have conjured up such grandeur! Winding our way up the barren, rocky cone of Mt. Lafayette, the surrounding mountains formed stupendous waves of blue, bluish-green and green, and we were walking on the very crest of one of them.

An elderly couple stopped us to inquire about my Alpenlite pack with its free standing frame. When the woman heard we had hiked from Georgia, she excitedly gave me a bear hug, pack and all. Imagine being hugged by a total stranger — the specialness of it all fit the day.

About six-thirty, exhausted physically but "high" spiritually and emotionally, we crossed a swampy col and found a flat campsite to the right of Garfield Pond. How good it was to lie down and rest.

September 6

Reflecting, I sat quietly in the early morning sunlight on the summit of Mt. Garfield and gazed upon all the peaks and valleys. The mountains silently shouted the Lord's words, "Be still and know I am God." Sereneness overflowed my soul, and the chorus of the hymn, "On Eagles Wings," echoed in my mind. I knew the Lord held us in the palm of His hand and would make us to shine like the sun. All we needed to do was to let His love shine through us.

The entire day was idyllic. Our Sunday dinner was prepared on a huge rock outcropping, a natural balcony on

South Twin Mountain, four thousand eight hundred feet above sea level. The atmosphere and scenery were superb and we agreed this was our best meal since beginning our journey.

The afternoon's hike was not as strenuous and we covered another six and six-tenths miles before finding a tent site amidst white birch trees and near a flowing brook.

September 7

At eight-thirty in the morning the AMC Zealand Falls Hut was practically deserted. Responding to our question concerning a place to purchase food, the hut girl suggested taking the A-Z trail into Crawford Notch, bringing us five miles closer to Twin Mountain town. Gene elected for us to go that way and he easily hitched a ride into town, leaving me and our packs behind at the hostel. A long time passed causing me to wonder if he'd find a way back. As it turned out, he had to pay a man ten dollars to drive him back, which would have been fine if the man had not been drinking. However, the man's driving verified his inebriated state and Gene experienced the greatest danger since beginning our trip.

While he was gone, I had time to deliberate on our noontime conversation, initiated by Gene's frank statement, "Time is running out. At the pace we are going, there's no way we can reach Katahdin on time." Although a vague awareness of time running out had crept into my consciousness since beginning the White Mountains, I was able to suppress it. Optimistic by nature, I kept telling myself that tomorrow we'd do better, but now that my leader had verbalized it, it became a reality and we had to deal with it.

September 8

'Love — it helps make everything beautiful.'

143

This is where our story began. Having relived the past five and a half months, the time had come to reach a crucial decision. Gene confided that there were many things he had begun in his lifetime but never totally finished. This was one undertaking he promised himself he'd complete in entirety. We both knew, though, given the circumstances and his partner, there was no way he could do this now without making a drastic change.

Although the idea of going separate ways admittedly saddened and distressed me, I offered to go home and allow Gene to complete the trail solo. Alone, I knew he could make it on time and I truly wanted him to have this privilege. Listening intently, Gene replied that he could not go on by himself. Physically, he agreed he could to it easily, but emotionally, he seriously doubted it. This Mountain Man needed his Wildflower! As much as he hungered to complete the trail, to reach Katahdin's summit alone would not satisfy him.

Unburdened, we cried together, each knowing the pain of loving too deeply — each realizing the finale would be different than we planned. Only our dream remained unchanged. We resolved to continue together, travelling as far as possible, and hopefully finding a way to answer Katahdin's call before going home together.

With our decision made, we scrambled up Webster Cliffs, arduous in places, with light happy hearts, expressing our love for one another with smiles, kisses and clumsy squeezes. It's awkward hugging with packs on! Skirting the edges of the cliffs, high above Crawford Notch, I felt like shouting from this mountaintop, telling all the world how tremendous it is to love and to be loved!

Arriving at Mizpah Hut about four o'clock, we feasted on hot soup, homemade bread and carrot cake. The atmosphere was warm and friendly and Gene suggested we stay, if they could accommodate us. Fortunately, there were several cancellations, possibly due to the deteriorating weather conditions.

Lively conversations with a diversified group of people and laughter accompanied the simple, plentiful food served family style in the large dining room, dimly lit with propane lights. The carefree mood was broken by reports via a shortwave radio detailing rescue attempts to aid a middle-aged male hiker troubled with failing knees.

Everyone retired early, hoping the morning would bring sunshine. Rubbing my sore knees, I fell asleep listening to the steady hard rain on the roof.

September 9

Guitar music and a robust voice, singing a humorous song about the weather, aroused us. The topic at breakfast centered on the advisability of venturing forth. After hearing the eight o'clock weather report predicting clearing, the majority slowly put on their foul weather gear. About thirty feet from the hut, with mist eerily swirling about, we stealthily slipped past the sign that read, "STOP! In inclement weather, do not proceed beyond this point."

Progress was slow. These unyielding mountains cut our hiking time in half, just like the southbound hiker predicted. The fog began to lift in places and scenes manifested themselves for brief spells. These flashes of blue sky and sharp images never failed to fascinate me. On Mt. Clinton, the relentless winds knocked Gene over and ballooned out my yellow rainlegs. Several times we huddled behind boulders and scrubby bushes to catch our breath. Choosing to circumvent Mt. Eisenhower, we stayed on the Appalachian Trail, which does not go over the peak.

In the proximity of Lake of the Clouds Hut, a mile and a half from the summit of Mt. Washington, presently hidden by clouds, the winds blasted us. Twice they slammed me in the back and I cried out, thinking I was about to be hurtled through the air. We staggered and struggled to keep our balance, and at last we reached the hut. Many hikers assembled there, unwilling to contest the ninety-miles-per-hour winds on Mt. Washington. Again, two more cancellations awaited us. We met Cindy Dresser for the first time and Mr. Howard, who we last saw at Muskrat Lean-to in

Georgia. The afternoon passed quickly as we talked and drank hot coffee and soup to keep warm. That night the winds moaned and the temperature dipped to ten degrees. Bundled in my sleeping bag, the day's events filtered through my mind. For me it was awesome staying above the timberline, knowing how quickly the weather could change and how devastating it could become. I found it inexplicably comforting to be encompassed by all these people and four stone walls.

September 10

'Mount Washington. A happy face is the best medicine. Keep smiling!'

Mt. Washington, normally engulfed in clouds, was totally visible, impassively waiting. The climb up was exhilarating and our spirits soared like Jonathan Seagull's in his moment of triumph. At one point, Gene turned and called to me, "I love you!" His cheeks were red from the cold and excitement; his blue eyes sparkled. We two were united in spirit and I could strongly feel my husband's tremendous love for me — a love deep enough to encourage me to reach new heights and experience the summits, allowing me freedom to grow. Without a doubt, we were on top of the world.

Like mortar, snow filled the spaces and crevices between the rocks. A simple wooden cross, wedged amongst the stones, starkly acknowledged the eighty-nine people who died assailing Mt. Washington. Seeing the weather station jutting into the blue skyline, we knew we were almost there. We arrived concurrently with a group of people who stepped off the cog railroad, which ascends the far side of the mountain. An eight-mile winding road permits cars to drive up and the cars displayed bumper stickers proclaiming, "This car climbed Mt. Washington!"

Inside one of the buildings, there were telephones, a restaurant, souvenir shops and restrooms. I never envisioned being able to call our daughter and parents from the summit of Mt. Washington, where the world's worst weather has been recorded, but we did. We even made reservations for the next hut.

Our afternoon was spent going over Mt. Clay and around Mt. Jefferson and Mt. Adams. Madison Hut was almost filled by the time we made our appearance. Consequently, only fourth level bunks were available. To my chagrin, this is one time I had to go to the bathroom in the middle of the night. Descending gracefully and noiselessly in the darkness was a farce.

September 11

During the last course of breakfast, the hut lady called for everyone's attention. Her grave expression and the urgency in her tone signaled that something was wrong and everyone listened. "We just received word two French hikers are lost in the area of Mt. Washington. We need volunteers to form a rescue party." Gene and I looked at one another and I could see his concern. Suddenly, shouting came from outside and the hut door flew open and a mountain climber, complete with coiled rope on his shoulder and French beret angled on his head, stomped in, loudly calling, "Pierre," and proceeded to jump from table to table. People smiled. At this point we realized that all the commotion was only theatrics, and Gene quickly sat down. This performance was the beginning of the traditional skit to teach the hikers how to "properly" fold their Appalachian Mountain Club blanket before leaving. By complying with this simple request, the hikers freed the limited hut personnel of an extra chore.

The climb over Mt. Madison was grueling for me. The mist was thick "pea soup" and we found our way over the rubble of rocks by following the cairns, guideposts made of more rocks. It was pick, pick, pick. My toes hurt, my knees hurt and I ended up with a tension headache from concentrating intensely on every step. Knowing that a hiker had only yesterday made a somersault over these rocks, miraculously landing on his pack instead of his feet and not injuring himself, made me even more cautious.

Was I ever grateful to get back into the woods on a pathway. Shortly thereafter we stopped to rest. Along came two men, first met in Lake of the Clouds Hut. Stopping to talk, one of them gave me his Lightning Bug Flashlight, weighing one-half ounce. He had let me borrow it the night we met and wanted me to have a flashlight for the rest of our journey. His thoughtfulness meant a light in the darkness.

At approximately six o'clock we reached Pinkham's Notch and the AMC camp, in reality a luxury hotel. Weighing our packs on the hook scale outside, Gene's weighted forty-eight pounds and mine thirty-six pounds, both only several pounds lighter than the day we left home.

There were vacancies but we had to sleep separately. My roommate turned out to be a research nurse working with psychiatric patients who had cardiac problems and were on the drug Tofranil. Gene's roommate was a man on a mushroom expedition with a group of people searching for various fungi.

After supper, Jack and Jean, a couple we met at Mizpah Hut, took Gene into Gorham to a laundromat. Not only did we have a hot shower and shampoo, but clean clothes.

September 12

Having heard numerous comments on the difficulty of the assault up Wildcat and the Three Wild Kittens, I felt apprehensive starting out and prayed for courage. However, I soon realized I could handle it and, feeling a surge of confidence, scrambled up Wildcat Ridge Trail ahead of Gene. It began to rain and we quickly put on our pack covers, omitting our rain gear as we were already too warm from exertion. As we mounted the third tier of ledges, the sun came out. Gene exclaimed, "There's a rainbow!" The rainbow was a magnificent arch of colors, below us, encompassing Pinkham Notch. I slipped out of my pack, as fast as possible, as it was precarious on the wet ledges. Gene held my pack from sliding, while I took four pictures. What a gift from the Lord! It had been years since we had seen a rainbow and never one from above it.

On Peak E of Wildcat Mountain, we passed near the Wildcat gondola terminal and watched some of the tiny cars slowly swing and sway as they ascended. Watching, riding up seemed to me far more daring than ascending on my two feet.

The weather changed hourly, alternating between cloudy, showers, clearing, sunny and misty. Descending steeply, by switchbacks, into Carter Notch, we met Jean and Jack leaving Carter Hut. They offered us their reservations as they found the weekend group too boisterous. Declining, we chose to go up to Carter Dome, camping in the pines one-half mile from the summit.

September 13

What a gorgeous day this was — blue skies, sunny, cool and windy. We paused on the open summit of Hight Mountain to take pictures of the Presidential Range. On South Carter Mountain, we heard soft cooing and turned to see two partridge on the trail, so engrossed in each other that they were oblivious to us. We met a young couple on Middle Carter Mountain, who had just finished climbing their forty-fifth four-thousand-foot peak in New Hampshire by reaching this mountaintop. The man was preparing for a marathon run in Rhode Island.

Middle Carter Mountain, Mt. Lethe, North Carter Mountain and Mt. Moriah consumed our afternoon. By six-thirty, saturated with fresh air, sleepy and ravenous, we set up camp in a boggy area. A gigantic orange full moon hung in the night sky. Tomorrow we would reach Gorham, New Hampshire, with only twenty miles to Maine!

September 14

At a junction, The Appalachian Trail turned onto the Rattle River Trail and descended steeply. The Rattle River noisily and forcefully rushed over, around and under the rocks in the riverbed. Its clear waters sparkled in the morning sunlight, dancing and tumbling in a frenzy. In several places there were large, deep pools that tempted us to jump in but the coolness of the September morning made us refrain.

Where the trail crossed Route #2, we were surprised to meet the two "California Girls," whom we had last seen in Pennsylvania. We talked briefly as they were anxious to be underway, having just come from Gorham. Fortunately, the 3.6 miles into Gorham were mostly downhill, since we were unsuccessful in our attempt to thumb a ride into town. Walking, though, gave us time to leisurely enjoy the stands of birch trees, aglow with yellow-gold leaves, that lined both sides of the road.

In Gorham we rented a room at the Alpine Tourist House, where each of us delighted in a hot shower, before we went looking for a restaurant. A Welsh Restaurant turned out to be the right place for us. A number of trips to the salad bar preceded our seafood dinner, which consisted of scallops and crabmeat in a delicate sauce with mushrooms and green onions — all very delectable.

Before retiring, a pint of ice cream each brought our day to a fitting close.

September 15

We enjoyed breakfast at the same Welsh Restaurant that we ate dinner in the night before and met a group of through-hikers there. Cindy, whom we had met at Lake of the Clouds Hut, and John from Tallahassee (last seen in Virginia) joined us at our table. Bob Barker, the senior hiker, who was hiking the entire trail despite the fact he had Multiple Sclerosis, stopped at our table to talk with us. This elderly man's courage and perseverance greatly impressed and inspired us.

Before departing from town, I called my brother, Bob, at his place of employment and discussed with him how Gene and I planned on hiking as far as we could before seeking a ride to Baxter Park. If the weather continued to be favorable and my knees held out, we hoped to reach Rangeley, Maine. Bob told me to call him when we reached that point, giving me the telephone number of the cottage he and his wife, Elaine, had rented on the Maine coast. They'd pick us up and drive us to Baxter Park and wait for us to climb Katahdin. The original plan was for them to meet us in Baxter Park after we descended Katahdin and take us to the coast for a gradual reentry into our fast-paced world.

The plans made, my brother connected me to my parents and then with our daughter and we had a three-way conversation. Hanging up, I experienced a warm, wonderful feeling, aware of how much my brother loved and cared about us, and how fantastic our support system was all along our journey.

Knowing the walk back to the trailhead was all uphill, we again tried thumbing a ride but the cars kept going past. After about ten minutes, a small car drove past us but then, astonishingly, backed up. The young woman driving said she never picked up hitchhikers, but we looked different. Squeezing into her car, we learned that Mona was on her way to begin a new job with the L. L. Bean Company. How happy we were to get back into the woods and be on our way again.

September 16 Maine

Gentian Pond Lean-to, complete with a wooden lounge chair, overlooked serene Gentian Pond. Although it was early, the loveliness of this place forced us to stop. Relaxing in the lounge chair, I considered the luxury of a backrest and smiled. Before our journey, I had taken such commonplace things for granted.

The hike to the New Hampshire-Maine borderline was a steep climb over several knobs and then up Mt. Success. Our arrival at the border was low key; we stood there, admiring the attractive sign, and contemplating the mileages, two hundred seventy-three miles to Katahdin and only fourteen days left. I felt numb inside; down deep I still wanted the impossible — I wanted to hike through to Katahdin; I felt disappointed in myself. With a little persuasion, I got Gene to pose for his picture alongside the sign.

Ten minutes later, we rounded a bend and faced a steep, deep, difficult rock obstacle course down. We maneuvered slowly and I felt on the verge of tears. Here we were, inching our way along, when I wanted to fly. Oh, how this trail teaches patience with oneself!

Beginning a steep ascent, Gene decided it was time to stop. We set up our tent in a thick cluster of pine trees, where the dampness, coolness and pine fragrance pacified our spirits.

September 17

The birds in Maine gave us a grand welcome! Flitting about, they awakened us as we felt their wings brushing against our tent. Later, I was fascinated to see a male spruce grouse, all shades of dark brown and black, pursuing a female grouse, warm brown in color, who was cooing lowly. His chest feathers were all puffed out and his chestnut-tipped tail feathers were fanned and erect. Scarlet eyebrows accented his black eyes, giving him a very distinct look.

As we crossed the open summit of Mont Carlo, two large, slate gray birds, about the size of pigeons and having white breasts, hovered around us, almost landing on our packs. They stayed with us until we dug out our camera, leaving at that point, as if camera shy.

The ups and downs were steep and we were weary by the time we reached Full Goose Shelter at lunch time. The setting was typical of what I imagined Maine to be like, copious pine trees, grayish skies, and cool weather.

Mistakenly, though, I thought Maine would be relatively easy.

We decided to climb Fulling Mill Mountain before camping, so as to be at the very beginning of Mahoosucs Notch, ready to tackle it when we were fresh and rested the following morning.

After we put up our tent, Gene searched futilely for water. As a last resort, he dug around in an area that looked moist and, digging deep enough, withdrew muddy water. He strained it through his wool sock and then boiled it. Lo and behold, we had safe water the color of rust. His woodsman's prowess never ceased to astound me, and again it was affirmed that he is truly a man of the mountains — My Mountain Man. Commenting on his well-chosen trail name, I considered my trail name, Wildflower, selected because a wildflower is simple and thrives in the rugged elements, providing it isn't trampled upon. A wildflower needs the respect of humans to survive.

It rained during the night and I dreamt I was in a large cathedral and there was a flood outside.

September 18

'Anything worthwhile is most always difficult. I love you.'

All the rumors turned out to be true! Mahoosuc Notch was a mile-long, boulder-strewn, dangerous passageway about one hundred feet wide passing between two vertical rock walls. Green velvet moss clad many of the rock obstacles, visually softening their hardness, but making them slick, while concealing deep crevices and holes. All this rock made it a very challenging but chilly place to be. There were even slender trees here, which surprised me as all I heard about were the rocks.

Upon entering the notch we at once began climbing, at times sliding, and other times crawling over massive rock formations. My Mountain Man pulled and pushed his Wildflower, as we labored and struggled together. In places I found myself alternately groaning and sighing. Our packs came off many times to facilitate maneuvering or squeezing through tight places and to occasionally rest and take some pictures. We marvelled at the sheer beauty of this notch and at its harsh demands. In several places white blazes directed the hiker into underground tunnels, having low ceilings. Concerned about damaging our pack frames, Gene chose to go over these areas and we slowly worked our way over, instead of under. One false move or wrong step could have resulted in an injury.

Muddy and scraped, we triumphantly emerged from the notch, feeling and looking exhausted but victorious. It had taken us six hours to hike one rugged mile! I felt certain we set a record for taking the longest!

September 19

Speck Pond, a scenic mountain tarn, was a delightful sight after our slick, toilsome climb up Mahoosuc Arm in the rain. Skirting its shoreline, we decided to eat lunch at the lean-to, where Mark, a through-hiker, was now the caretaker. He completed hiking the trail on August 17th and turned out to be the young hiker who yelled to us for directions our second day on the trail back in Georgia. Exchanging trail stories, he held our rapt attention, elaborating on what it felt like to nearly drown, having gone under twice while fording the Kennebec River, and telling his feelings hiking down from Katahdin. Sharing with this young man, time slipped away, while the weather turned colder and misty. Gene felt it was wisest to spend the night at the shelter and gladly paid our fee, one of the few places it cost to stay. Two men arrived, one of whom followed us since Georgia. His girlfriend aborted her hike in Gorham, New Hampshire. Two day hikers, well supplied with snacks, stopped and gave us each a crisp, juicy apple and cookie. Next John from Tallahassee appeared.

Late in the afternoon, with her poncho trailing like a queen's cape, Cindy, wet and muddy, made her grand entrance. It wasn't long before she was huddled in her sleeping bag trying to warm up.

A party of six weekenders from Vermont made it over Speck Mountain, heading south. Everyone moved closer together to make room in the lean-to. All the through-hikers watched, spellbound, as their leader began to prepare a gourmet feast in a manner rivaling Julia Child. The entree, artichoke hearts and clam chowder, made with real butter and milk, was followed by succulent lobster, rice, seven layer coconut cake, coffee, beer and wine. This incredible scene elicited oohs and ahs, good-natured banter and much laughter, along with some very real hunger pains.

Feeling ravenous, I finally had to bury my head in my sleeping bag.

September 20

'It may be difficult but with patience, the summit can be reached. I love you.'

Coming over the crown of Old Speck, the gusty winds howled, the rain was steady and the visibility poor. Where possible, we grabbed onto the low shrubs to keep ourselves from blowing over. With heads lowered, we slowly worked our way up, taking a step forward each time the winds momentarily subsided. Intermittently the rain turned to sleet, biting our faces. At one point, Gene was blown down and he resorted to crawling about thirty feet.

The summit seemed to evade us. It was there and then it wasn't; its elusiveness tantalized us. At last, we surmounted the acme. A dense grove of pine trees greeted us with swaying branches, like a group of friends with arms outstretched. Amidst them, stillness soothed us and we felt the protection of our friends.

Descending the north side of the mountain, we encountered Cathy and Craig, a young couple out for the weekend. Pausing to talk, they expressed amazement that we hiked from Georgia to Maine. Meeting them again at Grafton

Notch, Craig, "out of the blue," asked Gene if he could drive him to a store. Always hungry, Gene gratefully accepted this man's perceptive offer. The store turned out to be eighteen miles away. But Craig didn't mind; in fact, he took Gene to several stores to be certain he found all the necessary items. Two hours later they returned with two large sacks of groceries. Exchanging addresses, they bid us farewell, telling us to call them if we needed assistance farther along the way.

Each of us carried a bag of groceries in our arms, creating an incongruous picture as we headed back into the woods, where we happily set up camp behind a huge rock. Gene built a roaring fire, strung up our socks to dry and prepared us a hot supper. The Christ-like concern this couple expressed for us had ignited our spirits, and now the heat of the fire and food warmed our lean bodies, long stripped of any excess fat.

September 21

Our cold morning began with an unusual treat, a campfire. Last evening Gene had banked the fire and today, in a matter of minutes, he had created a cozy place for our breakfast in Grafton Notch. By now we knew that each time we went into a notch, the climb back out would be laborious. West Baldpate was no exception and after three and a half miles, we rested briefly before descending into a low sag and a small box canyon. Enchanted by its uniqueness, even though it was early, Gene suggested we eat lunch here, and we strung our space blanket between two trees to cut the winds, which howled above the trees. Enthralled by the lushness of our surroundings, an hour seemed like minutes. As we were repacking, we could hear someone coming. Cindy didn't see us so we called to her and invited her to sit down, have a granola bar and talk awhile. After conversing and taking pictures, Cindy hiked on ahead of us.

Reaching the apex of East Baldpate was easy and fun because of the flat slanted rock. Turning around, Old Speck loomed strikingly in the distance. Clouds of varying shades of white and light gray raced across the sky, forming an ever changing background for the Mahoosuc and Appalachian mountain chain, painted in full fall splendor.

In every direction we beheld our glorious, brilliant, beautiful world! Walking across the level surface of East Baldpate, we were ecstatic and moved to tears. Unlike other summits, there was no wind here — it was absolutely still and we shared silence with one another and our world. All this pristine beauty made us feel very significant! The Lord allowed us to be in this place, on this day, together, encircled by His rugged wilderness.

Yesterday, we struggled in the face of fierce winds and sleet; today, we basked in sunshine and silence and fall colors.

The day ended, as it began, with a crackling fire that sent sparks flying into the night.

September 22

The weather changed drastically and it became a cold, bone-chilling rainy day. For the first time in five and a half months, we spent the entire day in our five by seven tent as Gene felt it would be foolhardy to attempt to hike in this kind of weather. There'd be deep descents and, once wet, it would be impossible to get dry and to keep warm. The rules were different here in the north country in September.

Instead of hiking, we slept, talked and loved one another. By one-thirty we were famished, so Gene ventured forth to take down the food bag and we enjoyed cheese sandwiches, peanuts, raisins and M & Ms for a single meal for the day. Luckily, I had a pint of good water in my pack.

We reminisced a lot about our journey together on the trail and through life, feeling the Lord had a reason for slowing us down on this mountainside. Soon night came and I fell into a deep sleep, awakening several times to hear the rains pelting the tent. The continuous drumming of the raindrops mesmerized me and, in my twilight zone, I thought about how Gene always reminded me that we must have rain to fill the streams, of all the times we were thirsty in the drought-plagued states, and the "Cape Codder's" shrewd statement, "If you want to get to Maine, you must hike in the rain."

September 23

Rain, rain and more rain! Yes, it rained all day, letting up just long enough for Gene to prepare a hot breakfast before another deluge. Remaining in our tent for the second day, I read the Maine guidebook to Gene and we mentally hiked along until my voice lulled him back to sleep. With no one to talk with, I penned a seventeen-page letter to our daughter.

Mid-afternoon, I yearned for a cup of hot tea and with mild persuasion, Gene graciously prepared it, getting wet in the process, needless to say. Then, evaluating our situation, we placed the space blanket on the floor of the tent, attempting to keep things a bit drier. Having rearranged our tight quarters, we fixed prune sandwiches, which proved to be quite satisfying.

During the night we were abruptly aroused by exploding thunder and lightning. A terrible storm stalled overhead for hours before moving on and permitting us to drift back to sleep. But, then I awoke again to hear rushing water right beside my head. I had visions of a flash flood and in a panic shook Gene, who was himself wide awake. He reassured me we were high enough not to be flooded, but explained the spongy-type soil was saturated to the point that little rivulets were forming. I was unaware of his main concern, that of a leaning tree, pointed in our direction, and the real possibility of all the water totally uprooting it.

September 24

"When the waters become rough, STOP, THINK, as only then you can handle it. I love you."

With the first daylight, we began to pack, stiff from our two days of confinement and inactivity. Only a light drizzle fell now and we knew we had no other choice but to move on. This was the first time everything was wet, including our sleeping bags, which fortunately, were not down-filled.

The trail, slippery because of the exposed tree roots, fallen leaves and mud, followed a downward course. We began hearing sounds like water falls that grew louder all the time but we didn't know what to expect, as this recent reroute was not in our guidebook. Incredibly a stream had been transformed into a raging river, posing a different challenge. Again, nature had presented us with new terms and we either accept these terms or retrace our steps, which was unthinkable.

Taking off his pack, Gene went to scout the area, hoping to find a narrow crossing up farther, since we quickly learned we couldn't go downstream, where the river funnelled into a narrow place, sending boiling white foam down a natural flume into a gorge.

The situation was no better upstream and Gene, commenting, "This looks interesting," prepared for crossing right at this point. First he looped our nylon rope around a tree, shed his trousers, and in underwear, wool cap, boots and pack, slowly worked his way across, bracing himself with his trusty walking stick, while I looked on, fearful he may slip and be swept away. I cheered when he safely reached the other side and wrapped one end of the rope around a sturdy tree trunk, joining it securely to the other end of the rope with a double half hitch, giving us a double rope to hang onto and a means of retrieving the rope once across. Leaving his pack on the shore, he came back for me, having already told me to keep on my pack to increase my weight. Facing the ropes and gripping them with both hands, I inched my way across, having Gene behind me, helping me to remain upright, as the icy cold current rudely tugged at my boots and legs, trying hard to knock me down. Gooseflesh, caused by fright and cold, broke out on my body. We both realized the inherent danger in fording this river. Safely across, we sat down, with me feeling a little weak in the knees, to empty our boots of water and to wring out our socks. Only then did I laugh at my Mountain Man's attire.

We had yet another swollen stream to cross but it was rather level and not as threatening. Having crossed it, we soon reached paved Andover B-Hill Road, and we stood in the middle of the road, cold and wet, with water running out of our boots, uncertain in which direction the shelter was located. Here, my Mountain Man firmly announced, "This is as far as we are going!"

Moments later, a Wildlife Conservation truck appeared on the horizon and stopped to see if we needed assistance. Gene requested a ride into Andover and it almost seemed a dream to be riding in a heated cab, sitting between two men, while my husband sat in the open end of the truck, smiling broadly and freezing. The driver told me this was the worst rain they had had in over a hundred years and all the streams had become rushing rivers and advised us not to attempt continuing for at least two or three more days. He pointed to the turbulent river on our left saying we'd have to cross that. He let us out at Addie's Restaurant in the center of town and Addie directed us to Eva's, the only person in Andover who took in hikers.

Responding to our knock, a friendly, spirited elderly lady took one look at us and welcomed us in, telling us not to even bother removing our wet boots or packs. Taking us directly upstairs, she told us to select a room, instructing us to hang our wet sleeping bags over the banister, to run a hot bath, hang our rinsed-out socks over her stove and to make ourselves at home. Then she turned up the heat and we knew we would recover.

While I soaked in a hot tub, Gene went to Addie's to get something to eat before walking around the quaint town of Andover, taking pictures of the library and town hall. Coming back past Addie's, he spotted Cindy and hurried in to learn how she fared in all the rain. Cindy was with her parents, who picked her up at the shelter, with the intention of driving her to Baxter State Park so she could climb Katahdin before returning to her home in New York.

A very excited Mountain Man returned to announce we had a ride to Baxter State Park. The way was provided.

September 25, 26, and 27

'A positive attitude will most always remove the HOW from our minds. I love you.'

Three days were spent riding to Baxter State Park, all the while wishing I was still walking. Along the way we stopped in Rangeley to pick up Cindy's mail and, unexpectedly meeting John from Tallahassee on Main Street, picked him up also.

The first night, camped on the bank of the Kennebec River, Gene and I vowed to one another, one day we would return to Maine and complete the section of trail between Andover B-Hill Road and Katahdin Stream Campground in Baxter Park. The second night we camped beside Baussauc Lake, while the third night was spent encamped in an area just outside the entrance to Baxter State Park, since the Dresser's camper was too large to gain admission into the park. As always, my Mountain Man and I slept in our tent.

September 28

'At times it has been difficult, but, love, priority and determination have helped us reach our goal. I love you.'

Gene arose at dawn to find a cloudless sky. He easily aroused me, declaring, "We are going today!" Our excitement was sky high and contagious, and within minutes, everyone was up and final preparations begun. Cindy prepared a hearty breakfast while I packed our lunches. We even lit a candle for the table and converted a towel into a tablecloth as this was no ordinary meal.

Seeing a Class I Day posted, we all chanted, "It's a one!" This came as a total surprise as showers had been forecasted through Thursday. After signing the register provided at the ranger station in Katahdin Stream Campground, we were ready to begin.

Majestic Katahdin beckoned us. An unseen, but real "force," pulled me forward. The first two miles were fairly easy to climb but we proceeded slowly, savoring each step amongst the trees adorned in gold, rust and brown. I felt overly warm in my wool pants and for awhile regretted having them on, that is, until we reached the timberline. Here the air changed drastically, becoming cold and sharp.

Mixed feelings swept over me. I felt jubilant but sad. Six months had passed since we left home, an eternity that passed all too quickly. What would it be like to go home to my former way of life after living in the mountains all these months?

Once we reached the rocks, we laid down our walking sticks to be retrieved on our way down, as here they proved to be a hindrance, rather than a help. I almost felt guilty leaving it behind, as it had been my third leg all the way from Georgia. Hand rungs, made of one-half inch cold, rolled steel, were set in strategic places on the biggest rocks we had to scale. We four laughed a lot, pulling ourselves up and inadvertently getting ourselves into some comical predicaments.

The mist began to roll in and before long we were climbing in the clouds. We pressed on, seemingly climbing into nothingness. A hiker appeared, heading south, and we identified ourselves in the mist. He turned out to be Pete, whom we had last seen in Pearisburg. Learning who we were, he affirmed, "All right," and we spoke only briefly, eager to continue on. I thought of his friend, Lisa, who left the trail in New Jersey. And then I thought of Bob, one of the slain hikers, whose ashes had been sprinkled on this summit.

We met four day hikers who were turning back because of the extreme cold and hail. At this point we were about one and a half miles from the summit and I couldn't conceive not going forward, regardless of the conditions. In fact, a great surge of energy was spreading throughout my body; all my senses were fine-tuned. I anticipated the imminent climax, the crashing crescendo, the explosion of feelings, the celebration.

The plateau area, strewn with small rocks, had a lunar effect, and had rivulets of water and lots of wind. With the wind chill factor, I felt it was zero or below. We stopped to put on the rest of our clothes before the final ascent, helping each other as the winds were fierce. I now had on five layers consisting of T-shirt, flannel shirt, wool sweater, down jacket and rain jacket, wool cap and hood.

I blinked my eyes to be certain as, almost unbelievably, the summit of Katahdin appeared! My Mountain Man grabbed my hand, squeezing hard, and hand in hand, together we walked the last fifty feet. Only the sign, marking the summit was visible. Everything disappeared. The moment was now!

We clutched each other and tears filled our eyes. I had thought I'd shout with joy but instead, a tremendous quietness flooded my being. I had thought our journey would end with a crescendo, but instead silence surrounded us. How fitting.

In silence, the mountains demanded our strength and in return gave us their strength; in silence, the trees gave us their protection; in silence, the rivers gave us their life-sustaining waters, refreshing us. In sharing silence with nature, our faith in ourselves, in one another, in our fellowman and in our God had been renewed.

In shared silence, unexpectedly, we had been healed.

In Conclusion

Three years passed before we were free to return to Maine to finish our hike. This time, though, we hiked south, beginning at the base of Mt. Katahdin on July 22, 1984, arriving at our destination, Andover B-Hill Road, in dazzling sunlight on August 16th.

Shortly afterwards, standing in the heart of Andover, the Town Hall bells (in disrepair in 1981) were pealing the hour of ten. Instinctively, I knew they were ringing for us, celebrating our accomplishment. At last, our dream was a reality!

We had learned the Appalachian Trail parallels life. It has
     peaks and valleys,
     joys and sorrows,
     exhilarating times and ordinary times,
     sunshine and rain,
     laughter and tears,
     healing and pain,
     and, as in life,
     the trail has a
     beginning and an end.
     Likewise, the end is a new beginning.

Mount Lafayette, NH
September 5

Lehigh Valley, PA (Death Mount)
July 22

Summit: East Baldpate, ME
September 21

Smoky Mountain, TN
April 22

Grafton Notch, ME
September 20

Box Canyon, ME
September 21

Becon Hill, VT
August 24

Mahoosuc Notch, ME
September 18

Watauga Lake, NC
May 14

Sinking Creek - Mount, VA
June 8

Deep Gap, VA - May 20

Mount Garfield, NH - September 6